Unlimited Options

Career Strategies to Last a Lifetime

Lily Maestas, M.S.W.
University of California, Santa Barbara

K E N D A L L / H U N T   P U B L I S H I N G   C O M P A N Y
4050 Westmark Drive   Dubuque, Iowa 52002

Dedication

I would like to dedicate this book to Lorelei and Jack Snyder who helped me get started and helped me finish. Thank you.

I would like to also dedicate this book in memory of my dear friend and colleague, Alex Jimenez, a great career counselor, an even better friend and the best 'S' an 'N' like me will ever find.

Cover image © Julien Tromeur, 2008. Used under license from Shutterstock, Inc.

Contents

Introduction   vii
Professional Self Model   ix

Part I Personal Assessment   1

Chapter 1 Your Professional Self: Creating a Powerful Career Presence   3
The Monster of the Unknown: Fear and Changes   15
Becoming a Career Consumer: Learning Where to Shop   18
Taking the Show on the Road: Marketing Yourself   19
Why Personal Assessment Is So Important   21

Chapter 2 Inventorying Your Interests: Integrate Your Interests with Work   23
Get Help from the Experts: The Strong Interest Inventory and
    What It Means   26
Visualizing Your Dream Job: Putting Fantasy to Work   30
Personality/Interest Inventory   37
Holland's Occupational Themes—Typical Characteristics   43

Chapter 3 Identifying Your Skills: Don't Overlook the Obvious   47
Communicating Your Assets: Developing a Skills Vocabulary   53
Log On to Your Current Skills: Dissecting Your Past   56
Responsibilities + Skills = Accomplishments: Add Meaning to
    Your Skills   60
Skill Classification   63

Chapter 4   Determining Your Work Values: Setting Priorities   67
Discovering What You Want: Values Clarification   71
When You Can't Have Everything: Looking at Choices   71
Smell the Coffee: Wishing Doesn't Make It So   74
The Company and the World It Operates In: Corporate Values   76
Values Prioritization Exercise   79

Chapter 5 Identifying Your Personality Style: Using It to Create Career Satisfaction 85

My World, As I See It: Personality Types 92

Knowledge Is Power: Working Effectively with Diversity 96

Personal Style Inventory 100

Personal Style Inventory Scoring Sheet 104

Personality Styles in the Workplace 107

Getting Job Market Research to Pay Off 110

Part II Exploring and Researching the Job Market 111

Chapter 6 Researching Your Options: Identifying and Targeting the Markets 113

What in the World Is Going On?: Global Issues 117

What's Good in the USA Is Good for Me: National Trends 119

Industry-wise, What's Hot? What's Not?: Industry Trends 121

What Can I Do for You?: Researching Specific Positions 125

Who Is Hiring, and How Do I Find Them?: Employer
    Research 128

Straight from the Horse's Mouth: Informational Interviews 131

First Things First: Decision Time 134

The Professional Self Model: A Three-Step Process 137

Part III Developing Your Marketing Tools 139

Chapter 7 Correspondence That Sells: Whom to Write To— Why, When, and How 141

Cover Letters 141

Thank-You Letters 145

Clarification Letters 149

Acceptance/Rejection or Counteroffer Letters 152

Query Letters 156

Questionnaire 158

Industry-Specific Materials 161

Chapter 8 Creating a Convincing Résumé: Use Your Database to Repackage Yourself 163

Ambitious Professional Wants Good Title: Career Objectives 167
Experienced Administrator Has Done Everything: Skills,
   Experience, and Accomplishments 169
What Format Is Best?: Functional vs. Traditional vs.
   Electronic 174
Whom You Worked for and How Long: Experience History 176
Enhancing Your Image: Selecting the Nonessentials 176
Beyond Degrees: Education 178
Putting It All Together: Effective Editing 179
Functional Résumé Format 182
Traditional Chronological Résumé Format 184
Electronic Résumé Format 186

Chapter 9 Interviewing with Confidence: Creating a Job-Winning Image 189

Creating the Sizzle: Establishing Your Experience and Skills 194
Selling What You Will Do for the Company: Adding Value to
   Your Candidacy 195
Stacking the Deck in Your Favor: Selling Yourself 198
Putting Yourself in Control: Basic Preparation 202
My Biggest Fans: References 207
The Time, the Place, and Looking the Part: Nitty-Gritty Common
   Sense 208
Fifty Questions Frequently Asked at Interviews 211
Sixteen Attributes Sought by Employers 213

Chapter 10 Negotiating: The Slow Dance of Job Search 217

Send Up a Trial Balloon: Discuss Your Requirements 218
Put Your Terms on the Table: Presenting Your Plan 220
Thank You, But May We Talk Some More?: Introduce the
   Remaining Topics 221
Identify Your Allies: Who Will Make the Decision? 221
What Have You Gained? What Have You Lost?: Evaluating the
   Counteroffer 223
Head 'Em Off at the Pass and Call in the Big Guns: Identify the
   Road Blocks 225

Put It in Writing: Follow Up 228
Common Negotiable Items 230

Chapter 11 Establishing Your Time Line: Setting a Realistic Schedule 233
Don't Jump Ship: Employed People Make Stronger
  Candidates 235
Help Is Out There: From the Feds to Your Next-Door
  Neighbor 236
The Awful Truth: There Ain't No Free Lunch 238
At This Point in time: Determining Where You Are and What You
  Need to Do 240
Checkpoint Charlie: Keeping Yourself on Track 241
All Work and No Play Makes You-Know-What: Take Time to
  Smell the Flowers 243
Estimated Time Line for Career Changers 244
Estimated Time Line for Active Job Seekers 246

A The Role of the Career Counselor: What to Expect 249
Rethinking Your World: Act II 250

B When and How to Use an Employment Agency 253

Index 257

Introduction

FAST! One word defines the world you will enter upon completing your education. Fast not only means moving at a rapid pace; it implies a workplace dependent on creativity and innovation of ideas and services so that a company or organization can retain first position in the economy during times of relentless change. To insure your place in this fast world you have to take control of your career; unlike for your parents or grandparents companies no longer have designated career paths to follow. The new logic of careers lays the burden at your feet --- shaping your career is entirely up to you and how you choose to use the resources and guides you have access to or encounter along the way. Even though young adults, today, appear to be delaying their attachments to the workplace by pursuing a variety of activities to determine how they "fit" in the world of work, your planning and development begins the instant you step on campus that first day in the fall of your freshman year. Preparing yourself for FAST begins now! *Unlimited Options: Career Strategies to Last a Lifetime* is one tool that will make this process more effective and successful for you. Within the pages of this book are easy exercises that help you define who you are as a working person and how you want that manifested in the world or work.

In my career classes, two fictional characters are used to illustrate the quest one is on to find their calling or passion. Frodo, in this journey to destroy the ring, and Santiago, the shepherd in The Alchemist searching for his treasure, both learn from books but more importantly through engaging the world around them and learning from their experiences. Interestingly, they do not make the journey alone. They have guides and mentors to help along the way. As you will find out in your travels, individuals will step forward to assistant at important times. Some will provide the information contained in this book; tasks, insights, and plans that will provoke you to question where you are going, stimulate your engagement in what your university or college has to offer, and provide a resource that you can call upon again and again should your journey be visited by set-backs or misdirection's. You can pick and chose the materials and suggestions offered in here as your needs dictate. Once you gain confidence in your competencies and gain understanding as to the career choices you wish to pursue, this book will increase in value.

But we can not be only worried about what DeWitt Jones calls the "outer edges" of ourselves. These are the skills we hone in class as we master our discipline of choice and the additional skills we develop through practice in study abroad, lab work, internships, and civic engagement. Our outer edges get us only so far. We also have to hone our "inner edges" by gaining an understanding of who we are, and what we value at work, at home, and at play, and what we are stimulates our passions. Be honest during these reflective exercises – come back to them annually as you gain insights – offered throughout the book. This is hard; at least for me it is hard. Yet what you can achieve during your life is so much greater with some preparation and guidance.

This book has been created with you in mind. Each day you can have a dialogue with a peer through the stories that are shared. Begin to create your own story. Be open to the possibilities. Soon you will cross the stage with your diploma. Having prepared yourself you can now put yourself out into the world and know that you will embrace numerous opportunities and rewards.

Phil Gardner, PhD.
Director
Collegiate Employment Research Institute
Michigan State University

PROFESSIONAL SELF MODEL

THREE-STEP PROCESS

1. PERSONAL ASSESSMENT
2. DEVELOPING MARKETING TOOLS
3. RESEARCHING JOB MARKET

PERSONAL ASSESSMENT
- INTERESTS
- WORK VALUES
- SKILLS
- PERSONALITY STYLE

EXPLORING & RESEARCHING JOB MARKET
- GLOBAL & INTERNATIONAL TRENDS
- NATIONAL ISSUES
- IDENTIFYING INDUSTRIES
- ORGANIZATIONS WITHIN IDENTIFIED INDUSTRIES
- POSITIONS WITHIN THOSE INDUSTRIES

DEVELOPING MARKETING TOOLS
- RÉSUMÉS
- INTERVIEWING TECHNIQUES
- NEGOTIATION STRATEGIES
- CORRESPONDENCE
- INDUSTRY-SPECIFIC MATERIALS

DEVELOPING YOUR PROFESSIONAL SELF
AN OVERVIEW

PART I	PART II	PART III
ASSESSMENT	RESEARCH	MARKETING
•	•	•
IDENTIFIES YOUR PROFESSIONAL SELF, WHO YOU ARE, WHAT YOU CAN DO	EXPLORES COMPATIBLE MARKETS WITH YOUR PROFESSIONAL SELF.	DEVELOPS THE TOOLS TO REFINE, ESTABLISH, AND PRESENT YOUR PROFESSIONAL SELF.

Based on: Maestas, Lily, M.S.W., and Lorelei Snyder. *Unlimited Options: Career Strategies to Last a Lifetime.* Prosperity Press, Santa Barbara 1996.

Part I

Personal Assessment

1   Your Professional Self
Creating a Powerful Career Presence

*"Your Professional Self is an attitude, created through knowledge,
focused through research, and packaged to sell."*

Once upon a time, career change was pursued mainly by
unhappy, unfulfilled workers looking for more satisfying
opportunities. No longer. In the past few years, the employment
picture has turned topsy-turvy. "Downsizing" brought with it not
just the loss of jobs, but entire career paths. Technology is the
driving force that continues to redefine how labor is and will be
used, according to Phillip Gardner, Collegiate Employment
Research Institute. Manufacturing is moving offshore. Just as the
Baby Boomers thought they had arrived, many were ushered out
the door. Many more expect to leave their jobs soon, either
because they hate them or because they expect to lose them. The
over-fifty-five crowd is increasingly entertaining second and even
third career options as they take a serious look at redefining
retirement. Economic downturns, industry scandals, and
increasingly more competitive global markets have all made
workers of every age a little skittish when it comes to job security
and longevity in the job market. Young workers now realize they
will continue to receive "job training" the entire length of their
career and that security will happen as they are able to retool, adapt
to a changing market, and find their own place in a global
economy.

A university student planning to become the kindergarten
teacher at her old elementary school will face a classroom very
different than the one she was in. Technology will make it possible
for every student to use computers at their desks; most students
will begin their elementary school years with a working knowledge
of how to navigate online or run a computer program. Many of the
students will have multicultural homes where English and other
languages are spoken and interchanged at will. These children will
have a more global view of their existence than our young teacher
in training, whose parents and grandparents may have lived in the
same town. Her future students frequently travel from the United

States to visit their country of origin and understand and acknowledge the economic and social differences in a way that generational citizens of the United States can only imagine. We have to train ourselves and our students to become "global learners." We have so much more knowledge regarding learning styles, intelligence quotient, cultural values, and how they can be used to motivate and stimulate learning that this new teacher must prepare to be not only the educator, but the student willing to learn and incorporate what her international classroom has to share with her.

And so it is with all professions. Career change is in the air, for its own sake, out of necessity, and because people want and need change to grow and reach goals they have set for themselves. Even before the downsizing implosion, people changed jobs on average seven times and changed careers three times during their lives. Today that figure is much higher, and I am happy to report the American worker has begun to get comfortable with the notion of career mobility and the idea of multiple careers throughout his or her lifetime.

To be successful moving from one career to the next, you must take control of your future. You must develop and become comfortable with what I call your **Professional Self,** which you create for yourself through attitude, perspective, lifestyle choices, positioning, and planning.

College graduates begin their working lives with all kinds of dreams about what they want. How will it be for them in the world of work? Impressions from those around them shape their ideas of what kind of work would best suit them. For Mom and Dad, something with a fancy title and a little prestige, please. For your professor, that coveted spot in a Ph.D. program, where he hopes you will continue the research you started in his lab. For your friends, perhaps something that sounds dangerous and with lots of adventure and opportunity to travel would be what they picture for you. However, not one of them can truly know what you really want to do. In reality what you really want to do is to maybe take one more quarter of classes to make sure you feel ready. You're not ready to leave college yet.

How did this all happen so fast? Last time you looked, you were a junior and had plenty of time to think about this. Now it is spring quarter of your senior year, and graduation looms large. Your thoughts on the subject usually focus on the terror you feel at the thought of letting everyone down because you haven't got a clue what you are going to do after graduation, and everyone really seems to think you should know. They stare at you expectantly across the holiday table waiting for you to utter those words they have all been waiting to hear:"…I am currently reviewing several very good offers with lots of opportunity and I will let you know soon." Instead, they get some gobbledygook about wanting to keep your options open and wanting to make sure you pick the right thing. You're sitting at the holiday table talking about your future using all the euphemisms you can think of to stave them off till it's time to exit. Aunt Patty gives your mother's hand a comforting pat, and everyone gets back to the turkey as you settle into your chair and wait for your heart to stop racing and your ears to return to their natural color. You manage to get past them this time, but they will be back. Next time, be ready for them.

What you will find in this book are ways in which to provide you with the information, insight, and self-knowledge to be able to define for yourself and anybody who is willing to listen who you are as a Professional Self and what you want work to be for you. Is it going to be a full-time career endeavor that you will dedicate heart and soul to, or will it be a series of positions that teach you new things maybe provide travel opportunities or allow you to work part time? However it is that you chose to define your Professional Self, it is up to you to define that Professional Self in the most confident, self-aware manner in order for you to provide your livelihood.

Think about that for a minute. What do I mean by livelihood? I mean, how do you support your lifestyle? Is your lifestyle the reflection of what you need and is really important to you, or is it a reflection of what you should want based on the latest poll or article in *Architectural Digest*? Are you living the life you really want, or are you playing your life by somebody else's rules?

I take a moment to reflect on the day a Hospice social worker came to speak to my class about what he does for a living; he spoke not only from a career perspective but in a reflective what's-it-all-about perspective. What he said to the class has remained with me as one of the most profound things anyone has ever said in my presence about living a genuine life. Sam Leer, LCSW, spoke to my class about his job, sitting with people who are actively dying as they review the events that have made up their lives. He has spent the better part of this adult professional life tending to the near-death person, and his observations can provide clarity to the living. Mr. Leer told my class that the saddest part of his job is sitting with someone at the end of his or her life who realizes he or she has lived somebody else's version. The room was absolutely silent when he said that and remained so until I was able to take a breath and venture forward. My students reaction to the idea that at your death you realize that this is your one chance to be you and that you have spent all of it being who they wanted you to be must be was visceral. Their hearts were literally beating out of their chests as they engaged him in a emotionally charged discussion about what living a quality life means and how each of us must determine what it means and try to accommodate as much of that as possible within the confines of the other selves (e.g., spouse, parent, worker, etc.).

We begin our working lives with a somewhat undefined image of who we are and what we want professionally. Most times, our Professional Self is no more than an aura or ghostlike figure that has some tenuous boundaries but not much substance. Typically, it begins with the field we originally chose and trained for in college, with very little thought as to how this would wear in the long term.

*"Why are you here?" I asked the tall, blond, impeccably tailored professional I first met during college career counseling sessions four years earlier.

"You aren't the only one who wonders," Ellie Fairchild began. "It looked like I had it all, didn't it; like a dream come true. There I was, bright, good-looking, eager, five major companies clamoring for my favor." She paused a moment. "I made a good choice. The company believed in me, put me on the fast track, and I've doubled my salary since I've been there."

"So what's your problem?" I asked.

"I don't like retail, or at least I don't care about it. I'm manager of Accessories now. I have personnel and budgetary responsibility, I can see all the way up the career ladder; Mom and Dad are so proud they can't stop talking about their 'corporate climbing daughter.' My problem is I just can't see myself doing this for the rest of my life. When I think about it, it feels like a nightmare. I have no passion for what I am doing. Look, I know I am good at this. I can always work my way up another corporate ladder somewhere. What I want is a chance to be adventurous with my career. I want to try something in a totally new realm and see if I can do well there."*

Your attitude toward your current career and about change is the single most powerful tool you have.

Your attitude has a tremendous impact on your ability to control the outcome of your life. Viktor E. Frankel, author of the book *Man's Search for Meaning*, and a Holocaust survivor, describes this most vividly for me.

After a relatively charmed life as a noted and respected psychiatrist in the Europe of the twenties and thirties, Dr. Frankel found himself stripped to the naked existence of Auschwitz and Dachau. Every circumstance in the concentration camps conspired to make the prisoners lose their sense of self. The camps took away their clothes, shaved their heads and made them live communal lives, all in an effort to erase their individuality, their humanness— erase what made each of them unique. All familiar goals in life were snatched away. All that remained was their ability to "choose one's attitude in any given set of circumstances." Those who survived and went on to live productive lives never surrendered their attitude. Attitude became a basic survival skill. How we choose to feel about a given set of circumstances will say a lot about how we will proceed. If you look at the glass of water and see it half empty, then the events of your life will be painted with that brush; however, if you see the glass as half full, that too will affect the decisions you make and the outcome of your efforts. For me, the optimal word in Dr. Frankel's concept is not really "attitude" but rather how you "choose" to feel. When you perceive choices, or the idea that you can choose your attitude, you give yourself power. It may be the only power you might have in some instances, but you consciously retain some margin of control, perhaps not always over your circumstances but ultimately over how you choose to feel.

Although not as dramatic as Dr. Frankel's situation, starting your professional working life, changing careers, losing one's job, becoming disabled and unable to do the work you love, or simply hating what you do can be as devastating to our personal sense of worth. The concept of attitude often becomes obscured when you are confronted with a change you don't want to make.

One of the first things we ask someone we meet for the first time is, "What do you do?" A lot of times, our self-esteem is based on other people's reactions to our answer to that question, particularly for someone who has been "doing" the same thing for a number of years. The tremendous impact on our ability to interact successfully after losing a job stems from no longer being who we used to be. Most recent graduates fail to realize the impact their degree will have on their personal identity. For the first time since kindergarten, and for some nursery school, they are on longer students. They have been comfortable, even thrived in their identity as student. The world dealt with them under certain predictable parameters for over sixteen years leading up to their degree. You might even say that college graduates are the ultimate picture of the successful student.

The reality is that the day after graduation can be very traumatic for young adults. Now what? The question hangs heavy in the air of your parents' home as you take up residence once again to give yourself time to figure out your next move. Much has been written about the "quarterlife crisis" that young adults experience as they try to forge a life for themselves in their twenties. After years of observing this happen over and over again to our best and brightest as they emerged from the educational cocoon into the "real world," I felt compelled to write this book to offer some guidance for those willing to take on the challenge of forging their own lives; those willing to take control for how they will define their Professional Selfs and how that will be played out in the employment milieu.

Go ahead and mourn the loss of this identity, but along with that, begin to look at what this change can "do" for you. Take a realistic look at what you want from your next employment situation, and approach it with the attitude of choice and personal power.

Kathy Sims, former director of UCLA's Placement and Career Planning Center, believes three essential personal qualities are needed to be a successful career changer.

First, you must judge your level of hunger. Are you passionate for change? If so, you must channel that passion. Here's where attitude comes in.

What is your quotient for taking risk? You will have to develop strategies to accept the consequences as well as the rewards for that risk.

And finally, you must be able to be yourself and maintain perspective.

"Perspective is the real ticket," she says, and I agree with her.

> *Your must broaden your perspective; open your eyes and see what choices are out there. What information are you overlooking that could provide unexpected opportunities?*

Occasionally, we all need to take a look at things with a different set of eyes. Perspective gives us an opportunity to walk around a problem, look at it from different angles, and perhaps see what we haven't seen before. All too often, we get stuck in the familiar and are so comfortable with our discomfort that we settle, as opposed to venturing out of our comfort zone and risking at little. We need to take a global view of the economy and of its labor force when making career change. In studies conducted by the United Nations on education and employment trends globally, it is reported that 15 percent of the world's population hold bachelors degrees, and only 5 percent have advanced degrees. Think about this for a minute. As you ponder what choices you have as a college graduate, remember that you have more employment choices than 85 percent of the people that walk the face of the earth! It's not that you don't have choices, what you don't have is information to maximize those choices. National figures, available through the Bureau of Labor Statistics, indicate that the area in the United States with the highest density of college degrees is in the metropolitan Washington, D.C., area, with 48 percent of the adult population having a bachelor's degree. California is one of the highest, with 29 percent of its residents achieving degree status, and Mississippi at the lowest, with 18 percent of their adult population having bachelor's degrees.

In the process of gaining perspective, I have seen clients make better choices regarding their career path. Some have chosen to leave the degree-dense areas where the competition can be stiff and relocate to an area where they are a higher commodity in relation to the population in general. I have seen others choose to stay and develop stronger, more marketable skills in order to have the hiring advantage when everyone seems to be equally qualified. What ever your decisions may be in regard to career choice, make sure you have provided enough room for perspective so that your decisions are not made in a vacuum.

As you grow in experience, skills, and job-related talents, your Professional Self will begin to take shape, develop density, and become more complex and versatile. The idea of choices emerges as you take control of the path you want your working life to take. The image becomes clearer and sharper, not only to you but to the world at large.

> **Your Professional Self is an attitude, created through knowledge, focused through research, and packaged to sell.**

This can be one of the most exciting times in your life. You have the opportunity to begin afresh. Now is the time to look at your dreams. What have you always wanted to do? It can also be terrifying.

I asked Ellie why she didn't change. "What's holding you back?"

"Do you have any idea how much my dad paid for my college education to get me where I am?"

I nodded.

"What am I supposed to do? Throw all that away? And if I do, what would I throw it away for? How do I know the next thing won't be as disappointing as this?"

A major stumbling block for career changers is fear the next step won't be any better than what they're leaving behind. This concern is legitimate.

"Most people," says Gerald M. Sturman, chairman and CEO of Career Development Team, "find their jobs by hitchhiking. There's very little in the way of real planning. As a result, most of us go through our careers with a vague sense of uneasiness." There are other fears. Fear you have nothing to offer. Fear no one will take you seriously. Fear your first job offer will be your only offer. There is no need to stumble and collapse over these fears. Through these pages, you'll develop a road map for identifying, finding, and getting jobs of your choice. You'll identify and prioritize your work values, giving yourself a framework for evaluating your options. You'll end up with an action plan for success.

Recently, I had a visit from Jim Murchison, a former student, who called to my attention an exercise I once assigned his class regarding the basis of our attitudes about work.

Oh yes! I remembered it vividly because Jim was so upset by what he learned that day.

I asked the class to complete the following statements:

1. My father's attitude about work is ...
2. My mother's attitude about work is ...
3. My biggest fear about becoming a working adult is ...

Through the exercise Jim recalled how much his father hated his job. He had worked for years as a production manager in an industrial firm. He felt stuck in a dead-end job, unappreciated by his employer and misunderstood by his colleagues. In short, his work life was lousy, and this feeling spilled over into his family and all other areas of his life. Although the job made him miserable, he kept at it because he felt he had to.

Jim's biggest fear was that what happened to his father would happen to him, and that he, too, would end up in a dead-end job, working for somebody he didn't like, doing something he didn't want to do, and being there for the rest of his life. As a graduating senior about ready to enter the workforce, it made the future terrifying.

As it turned out, several others in the class shared similar feelings.

"Often times, how much you enjoy your work and the degree of control you have over your work environment are directly related," I told them. Jim's father felt no control and believed himself a victim of his workplace.

"This doesn't have to be," I assured them. The better you know who you are and what you have to offer, the more control you have over the choices you make about what kind of work you choose to do, and where you do it. Work can be fun. You can be excited about the time spent at your place of business. You can define your life in positive ways through the kind of work you do and the pleasure you derive from it.

Jim had come back to tell me that after that particular day he had rethought his attitudes and readjusted his ideas of what work was going to be.

"Right after graduation, I got a job with a software company that designs computer games," he told me. "I'd always *been interested in computer games, but was afraid to look for jobs in that field because it didn't seem like 'real' work. You should have heard my dad when I told him. He couldn't believe I was serious."*

Jim was now in the research and development division designing computer games and had just been promoted for the fourth time in the last eighteen months. His salary had doubled, and he traveled extensively.

*"They call me the 'Boy Wonder,'" he chuckled. "I'm having the time of my life, doing what I love in an industry that fascinates me. And you should hear my dad brag about me," he told me as he left. ***

You'll find this book different in that it stays focused on the job search and career planning process; it organizes the process in a logical sequence and reinforces each step with consistent application. It's lean and mean, with no fat chapters on "The Job Market," "The Numbers Game," or "The Psychological Trauma of Looking for Work." Each chapter concentrates on a single step, illustrated by a single case study. This method was chosen to show you how my clients have struggled with these problems, worked them through, not without difficulty, and seen their persistence and planning pay off. You can, too.

Each chapter builds on previous work, moving from personal assessment, to research, to marketing yourself. Each subject uses previous skills in conquering the next step, giving the total process a down-to-earth, this-is-how-you-use-this-information emphasis. Through easy-to-use exercises, you'll learn to identify those skills and experiences in your own background that make you a "value adding" candidate to any organization you choose to affiliate with.

This step-by-step process is not for everyone. Each of you enters the career planning process at a different point. Your needs are different at each point. This flexible plan stresses a process that is effective for beginning professionals and applies as well to those in their middle years and beyond. The information you need to make the process meaningful and productive changes throughout your lifetime. The entry-level professional contemplating changing jobs for the first time will have needs very different from that of a mid-level manager squeezed out by a corporate merger. Reentry women, persons with disabilities, and returning military will have different needs. If you need a résumé right now, go directly to that chapter. If you have an interview scheduled, don't wait for the rest of the book. Once you've addressed your most pressing need, think about the process in total and start at the beginning.

> *Most people go through life having their work dictate their lifestyle. I suggest that you shift your priorities to let your lifestyle dictate the work you do.*

Whose responsibility is it to determine what your lifestyle will be? If you want more leisure time, take a long, hard look at your finances, figure out how much money you can do without and what that will mean in terms of extras you might have to give up. You might also want to look at what you can do to work less and earn more. If you want more prestige or security in your work life, then you may have to seriously deal with the idea of retraining or going back to school to acquire the expertise you'll need to create that lifestyle.

I hear people tell me all the time how they love to travel but get only two weeks of vacation a year. What is wrong with this picture? If you want to travel, find an employer that offers blocks of time off, or better yet, find a position that requires travel. Learn another language, become a tour guide, apply for a job on a Semester at Sea cruise, teach English abroad and see the world. I know of one young man who wanted to see the United States at someone else's expense. He went to school and learned to drive sixteen-wheel tractor-trailers. And he always kept his fishing rod behind the seat. This may not be your dream job, but for five years it was his dream. And when he was ready for a change, he took out this book and started the process all over again.

When was the last time you actually thought about your "dream job?" Now is a good time to do that. Are you overlooking skills that increase your marketability? As you work through the process, you'll be collecting the information you'll need to put together strong résumés. You'll have organized your thoughts to impress the interviewer of the value you will add to that organization. You'll be prepared to negotiate for a higher salary, more challenging work assignments, and greater job satisfaction. You'll know a lot more about yourself and what makes you unique in the business world. You'll see choices and take control of your destiny. Feeling good about your work (it's that attitude thing again) vastly impacts your quality of life and the steps you take to get there.

The Monster of the Unknown
Fear and Changes

A key element of career planning is change. Our lifestyle needs change as our life experiences change. As a twenty-four-year-old right out of college, you may be much more interested in adventure than security, but as you settle into adulthood and gain the responsibilities that accompany it, your lifestyle needs change. The young truck driver married and had a family. Long-distance driving was no longer fun, and he moved on. In the meantime, he had traveled from Canada to Kentucky to New Jersey and collected a paycheck the whole time. When he was ready to settle down, he went to a community college that specialized in vocational education became a nurse and now is in charge of medical services for a major construction company in California. He hires, trains, and supervises medical personnel who by law must be on site at major construction areas. His needs changed, his lifestyle changed, but the process to accommodate those changes and secure meaningful, financially rewarding employment didn't change. It was the Professional Self Model all over again. The information he used was different, but the process still provided the venue for the exploration of values, skills, interests, and personality style as it relates to the job market.

Change by its very nature is stressful, to say the least. It requires you to make room in your life for new activities, to look at your life in new ways, and to take risks. Fear of the unknown, or of change in general, can hold you back, even when you know the odds are that change will be for the better. The biggest enemy for anyone who wants to change is inertia. Don't let it paralyze you into a stillness that causes you to accept the status quo and prevents you from moving in new, and potentially more rewarding, directions. This discomfort is normal and necessary to the creative process. Accept that, and keep moving ahead, one small step at a time. Before long, each small step adds up.

Some thoughts on change:
- All change is accompanied by some type of stress.
- Change is not a smooth-flowing process—it stumbles, stalls, delays.
- Change seems to involve the removal of old information before any new information is to be incorporated as a behavior—"Getting rid of old habits" as the say.
- The more we fail to recognize we are in a change situation, the more difficult it is to get through the change.

Four key actions to navigate change:

- Acknowledge your own reactions to change.
- Access the impact of the change.
- Seek and acknowledge reactions of others.
- Take positive action individually and with others.
- Develop coping mechanisms to deal with the stress.

Benefits of Change:
- Increased self-confidence
- New opportunities that may present themselves as a result of change
- Impact you have on other people
- Broadening of your expectations of what can be

For most college graduates, leaving the university may be the first time they truly strike out on their own. Once again the term "quarterlife crisis" seems appropriate for talking about this time in young adults' lives. Change will occur whether you want it to or not. You will be granted a diploma and in one way or another escorted off the campus. Your living situation for the last two years, sharing a two-bedroom apartment with four girls who have become closer than family suddenly comes to an end and you're forced to look for new housing—with strangers no less. No wonder the idea of moving home has some appeal. Student loans are coming due, and your excuse for not looking for work right after college is sounding really old. Your summer is Europe is almost over, and you are no clearer about what the future holds than when you hopefully dropped three coins into Trevi Fountain in Rome and wished for all your dreams to come true.

Here it comes: the end of the summer of your senior year of college. It's over; it's time to start…but start what? Don't be so afraid. You have succeeded at so many things in the past; it is just a matter of getting the right information, talking to the people who can help you, and deciding to take action. Own this job search and approach it with the same vengeance that won you the speech tournament when you were a freshman or when you landed that great research assistantship against the graduate student that you thought would easily waltz into the position. What about your interview with the Big Four Accounting firms the summer of your junior year? All of these are successes you can look back on and learn from. As you approach your next venture, the world of work, have a sense of adventure and be confident; it is your time and place to be here and be the best you that you can be. Taking action may sound frightening, but standing still and letting life happen is not what you came for. It is not what you invested thousands of dollars and hours of your time for. You are not the kind of person to sit still. With a little bit of information and some proven job search tools, you can find your place in the world of work. Not just once, but over and over again as the fates decide.

These chapters will help you overcome this natural reluctance. Each provides general information on a specific step in the process, illustrated by a case study involving a real person, who, like yourself, used this system to take control of his or her professional life. (We've changed their names and some personal details at their request.) These are not casual meetings. You'll have a chance to walk in their shoes and to get to know them very well. You'll be able to identify with their situations, their concerns, their frustrations, and their success. You'll see how to apply the theory and process to your own situation.

Taking stock of yourself is a most formidable task. It takes work, commitment, time, and patience. It creates an invaluable database, which gives you the power to pick and choose the interests, skills, and values you want to pursue and market in individualized job searches. The exercises and inventories quickly give you a picture of who you are as a working professional—a picture of who you want to be. You are no longer a passive victim. You have a good idea of who your Professional Self is. You have taken control. The words in this book will give you the process; they will give you the information you need to own your career. You will provide the action necessary to implement your well-thought-out plan.

Becoming a Career Consumer
Learning Where to Shop

"Give a man a fish and he eats for a day. Teach him how to fish and he eats for a lifetime." Here, you'll learn not only *how* to fish but *where* to fish. As a career changer, you'll learn to determine employment trends within industries, forecast job security regionally, and establish a way of thinking about your professional life that includes the entire world economy. In a world where car engines are made in Europe, the electronics are made in Asia, the body moldings and interiors are manufactured in Latin America, and the automobiles are assembled in the United States, it is naïve to assume you are not affected by the politics and economic climate of the entire world. As you develop your Professional Self, one of your most significant tasks will be to

18

learn to receive, screen, and interpret information in your role as a career consumer. It need not be difficult.

As you become more sophisticated in this role, you'll soon recognize industries and career paths likely to expand and those that are on a downward path. With this "macroeconomic" foundation in hand and the information about yourself you've developed earlier, you'll be able to quickly eliminate unproductive areas. Once the elimination process is complete, what's left will direct you toward likely industries to concentrate on.

As you identify, research, and review these industries, firms, and positions, you'll develop your own criteria for benefits, organizational values, and goals that are important to you. You'll find this particularly beneficial when you reach the negotiation stage.

Taking the Show on the Road
Marketing Yourself

Résumés and interviews are simply marketing tools to help you sell yourself. You are the one who gets the job. The fundamental techniques you'll find here groom you to present yourself as a competent, capable person. Developing these tools gives you the self-confidence you need to convince the employer that you're worth what you're asking for.

Information is the key to unlocking your Professional Self and positioning yourself for the future you choose. You'll need not only information about yourself, the job market, and the economy, but information on job search strategies and the career-planning process. You open the door to new beginnings. Remember, the past cannot be changed, but the future is whatever you want it to be.

You can now position yourself to achieve the future you choose.

Each position you take in your professional life should provide you with the opportunity to learn new skills, challenge your existing ones, and prepare you to move on.

> ### *To reach your goal, you must plan your future.*

Consciously setting up three- to five-year plans that develop guidelines for what you want to accomplish in that time will give you a road map to follow. This is not to suggest that in setting up these plans you will achieve all your goals. I've lived long enough to know that life has a way of taking unexpected turns and creating situations you could never expect or plan for. But it's surprising how often these plans work. A colleague of mine was the assistant director of alumni affairs at one of our California state colleges. Her first five-year plan called for her being appointed a director of alumni affairs within that time. She identified the skills and experience she felt were needed for that position and set about acquiring them. After three years, the alumni affairs director unexpectedly accepted a new position at another school, and she successfully applied for the job. She's now on her next five-year plan, to become director of development, and is building skills and experience in that direction.

As my colleague did, use your three- to five-year plan to set your goals. If you are able to achieve only half of what you set out to do, think about all you'll have accomplished. And if you don't, well, think about that too. If you don't set out a plan for your life, who will?

Work should be an unending source of satisfaction, and here you'll find the concrete steps you need to identify where to look and what to look for to make this happen. Now you see your Professional Self in total. You know who you are, you know what you bring to the table, and you know what you want. You are now in a power position. Use it.

Why Personal Assessment Is So Important

- It identifies your Professional Self.

- It develops "raw data" for your job search.

- It enriches the vocabulary you use to describe your Professional Self.

- It lets you decide which skills, talents and traits you want to market, which you want to acquire, which you want to bank for another time, which you want to leave behind.

- It develops choices you never suspected you had.

- It creates a level of self-awareness that builds confidence in your ability to achieve

2   Inventorying Your Interests
Integrate Your Interests with Work

"You have the right to pursue meaningful work in an environment that is not only intellectually challenging, but in an area that you are drawn to."
Lily Maestas

Jonathan Banks was a solitary man with a dull job who harbored a secret desire for excitement. He reminded me a little of a Woody Allen character—slight of build, shy, awkward, and unassuming. He had always been a passive observer, content to sit back and let life happen to him. Now he wanted a change, but could not define, even to himself, what he wanted that change to be.

* *"I graduated from college in 1998 with a double major in music performance and mathematics. The two are not as disparate as they might seem,"* he answered my surprised expression. *"Music is a very calculated kind of art made up of things like bars, notes, scales, and measures."*

When he left school, he zeroed in on his math skills as his only employable option and was quickly hired by an insurance company as an actuary, computing insurance risks and premiums. His success was predictable, given his pedantic nature, and he went on to get his certification.

"I'm twenty-eight years old. I earned $92,000 last year. I've managed to accumulate a significant savings account, an attractive investment portfolio, and a great condo. I'm not really unhappy," he shrugged. *"I just seem to be in a rut, and I want to get out. I want something more exciting. Working as an actuary is exceedingly independent work; there is little interaction with other people, and if I stay here, I'll never be involved with people."*

"Is that a problem for you?" I asked.

"Actually, the real problem is that it's hard for me to make friends outside the office," he confessed. *Now, five years into his career, he found himself lonely as well as bored. He knew he needed to find the social interaction he craved in his work setting because his shy and retiring nature made it too difficult to generate this for himself during his leisure hours. *

A good place to begin defining your Professional Self is with your hobbies and special interests. Career changers should particularly look for opportunities to combine those interests, hobbies, and talents with the job market to create a work experience that excites them.

Your work should stir you up. It's important when making career choices to think about what creates that stimulation for you. We all spend the majority of our adult lives involved in some sort of employment venture, so why not try to make it pleasurable? I'm always surprised at how few people do this and amazed that so many believe that work needs to be tedious, a drudgery, a bore. Exploring your interests is one of the best ways to begin the excavation of your experiences thus far, so we can begin to identify those areas or activities that were of special interest to you. From there, we can take a look at some of the industries that support those interest areas of yours and where there might be employment opportunities. Right now, this may sound like a far-fetched process, maybe a little abstract. That's because it is new to you, and anytime we learn new ways of doing things there is bound to be a learning curve. Once we explore several of your experiences, you will understand how to pick through your life for key elements that will make up the interests for your Professional Self.

You have a *right* to pursue meaningful work in an environment that is not only intellectually challenging but in an area that you are drawn to. You can and should include your outside interests and hobbies as you begin to explore employment opportunities.

One of my student clients demonstrates this profoundly. She was a national surfing champion who was graduating from our College of Creative Studies, where she had won several writing competitions. Faced with the need for a job, she couldn't seem to move ahead. Frustrated, I finally slammed my hand down on the table and demanded, "What is it you want?"

"You really want to know? I'm tired of school. All I want to do is hang out with surfers."

"All right. What skills do you have, aside from surfing, that are appropriate for that?" Because of her writing credentials, she began researching magazines. At the time there were seventeen surfing magazines in this country, seven of them in California. Three invited her for interviews. She returned to me after one of them.

"This is the place for me! I got there at nine o'clock, but no one was there, and the place was locked up. There was a sign on the door that said, 'Surf's up. Be back at noon.
If you want to interview, we have a wet suit for you and we are at the Rincon. See you there.' That's my kind of place to work!"

And sure enough, it was. But not forever. After two exciting years, traveling the world writing articles about surfers, surfing, surf boards and any other angle on surfing she could think of, she was ready to move on. As with our truck driver friend in chapter one, she went through the process outlined here and made some decisions regarding her next career move. Her needs changed, her values changed and she wanted a change in lifestyle. She applied all of this new information to this process and was ready to move on with a well laid out plan. She applied to several MBA programs, graduated from Stanford several years later, and last I heard was firmly ensconced in corporate America in the TransAmerica building in San Francisco.

Although making a change was important to him, in his very measured way, Jonathan wanted to scientifically approach this career search so that he had to make only one switch. As Jonathan saw it, the way to do this was to get the help of a professional career counselor who would tell him what to do with the rest of his life. Not so! Career counselors can only guide. How successful Jonathan was depended on how willing he was to act on that guidance. I made no bones about that.
"Have you thought about moving to a different industry that would provide you with a more interesting lifestyle?" I asked.
"I can certainly see myself using my mathematical skills and my computer skills, but to be an actuary, you have to pretty much be in the insurance industry," he replied. Jonathan's

attitudes about work were not negative so much as they were self-limiting.

Getting Jonathan to talk about what excited him was difficult. I kept trying to draw out what excited him, and initially he could think of very little. He was very reticent to do any kind of testing.

*"I've done these things before, and I never know what to do with the results. It's just been a waste of time." ***

Get Help from the Experts
The Strong Interest Inventory and What It Means

One way to define interest areas and relate them to job opportunities is through the Strong Interest Inventory (SII). The premise here is that people in a particular occupation usually have similar likes and dislikes, and how much they enjoy their work comes from those interests and the relationships they develop with their co-workers. It stands to reason that if the people you are working with have similar interests, likes, and dislikes, you will be more likely to develop comfortable, compatible working relationships with them, and therefore get a greater degree of satisfaction from your work. Career research has shown that people often measure their "degree of satisfaction" about their jobs by the quality of relationships or the people they work with.

The SII is based on six occupational themes as defined by John Holland, author of *Making Vocational Choices* and one of the internationally known experts on career development theory. The inventory presents you with a series of activities, occupations, and characteristics. You respond whether you like, dislike, or are indifferent to them. Your replies are then compared to sets of people in a number of occupations to determine compatibility. If your responses are similar to, say, travel agents, you can assume that you have a greater chance for job satisfaction within that particular occupation than in one where you had nothing in common.

Most career centers at community colleges and private career counselors offer this inventory and interpretation for nominal fees. If you don't have access to a career center or a career counselor, you can test yourself with Holland's Self-Directed Search. It's easy and fun and comes with instructions for use and interpretation. The test is published by Psychological Assessment Resources, Inc. (Call 1-800-331-TEST toll-free for information). Or go online at www.parinc.com. You can use the modified version, developed by Betty Neville Michelozzi, included here.

The results of the SII are broken down into six occupational themes: Realistic, Investigative, Artistic, Social, Enterprising, and Conventional. Based on the results, you are given a three-letter code, which indicates the three occupational categories where you were most compatible. For example, if your three strongest areas of compatibility were Investigative, Social, and Enterprising, your three letter code would be ISE.

*"Standardized tests won't tell you what you should do," I told Jonathan. "They will give you and me a general direction from which to focus your occupational search. You initially told me you didn't want to experiment with a lot of different professions; you just wanted to make one decision and have that be a good decision," I reminded him. "Rather than asking you to try this and try that, let's take a look at what the SII indicates your areas of interest are, and then let's use that as a road map that gives us some direction but helps us eliminate whole areas where you show no interest. Let's begin to formulate a plan based on the information we get from this inventory. And if nothing else, we are going to find out what areas we can quickly cross off because you're not interested in them. What we want to find out is what kind of industries and what kind of work responsibilities are going to generate some measure of excitement for you," I said.
When he returned the following week for an interpretation of the results, like many of my clients, he couldn't see the relevance of the results. Despite my disclaimers, he viewed this as an aptitude test and fully expected it would give him six or seven professions he would be "good" at. *

So many people say, "I took the SII, and it said I should be a financial analyst," or a lawyer, or a whatever. The fact is, this inventory is not designed to identify *aptitude* or *competency*, but rather to identify occupational *interest* categories, indicating your compatibility with professionals in those occupations.

That's all. The Strong Interest Inventory is not a list of occupations that you will be "good at"; it is rather meant to cover the person/environment fit. What occupations will hold your interest because the work provides the kind of environment that is conducive to providing strong working relationships? That is more what the Strong is all about. The information provided by the Strong is best used in conjunction with some career counseling or at the very least some reading on the part of the career seeker regarding how to interpret the results of the Strong Interest Inventory. Used for its intended purpose, it can be a valuable resource in career exploration.

The results do not indicate your talent, skill, or experience with any of them, or that you have the necessary skills, but rather expands your avenues for further exploration. Look at the results of the SII as a road map that widens the highway as you move toward your career objectives.

When looking at your SII results, it is important to look at occupations in all of the themes of your code. This will give you the broadest variety of work environments, industries, and positions to explore.

*   The three strongest occupational interest areas for Jonathan were Investigative, Artistic, and Conventional. This was not surprising to me. The Investigative fell right in line with his math background. Investigative types generally prefer to solve abstract problems and try to understand the physical world rather than act upon it.*

The Artistic area validated his interest in and love of music, and his aptitude and ability to perform in a musical environment. In college, Jonathan had trained as a performance artist, but he chose not to pursue this because music performance felt a little too out there for Jonathan. He preferred to work alone, although he had a great need for individualistic expression and described himself as independent, original, and expressive.

As a direct opposite to these other two was the Conventional part of Jonathan that preferred highly ordered activities that he controlled. This again confirmed what we already knew about him. He did not like to be the leader, did not seek or want the limelight, and liked to know exactly what was expected of him. He saw himself as conventional, stable, well controlled, and dependable. *

In establishing this base for yourself, you are now in a position to determine what your next step is going to be, whether that is moving from one industry to another, looking more deeply into what you are already doing, or retraining to gain the necessary skills for a new occupation. Now that you have an idea of where to begin, you are better equipped to describe for yourself and others what kind of work you are looking for, in what industries, using what skills. Having an idea of where to begin feeds into greater self-confidence and control in the job search.

Next, we looked at occupations that Holland defines as falling into the IAC categories, giving Jonathan a starting point for his occupational search. Investigative people prefer occupations like programmers, chemists, psychologists, mathematicians, science teachers, college professors, and doctors. These types are curious and want to work in an area that involves significant amounts of problem solving. It may involve problem solving in medicine, academic research, law, or outer space—people who are investigative what to know the answers to "why?" The Artistic types tend toward teaching English as well as art, interior decoration, acting, writing, composing, photography, cosmetology, reporting, and advertising. Artistic types are creative with either their expressions or in their work. They are more spontaneous than methodical and usually have several projects happening all at once. Many of the Conventional types are happy as accountants, bankers, secretaries, credit managers, dietitians, and business education teachers. These Conventional types are the workers who truly do keep things going. They are the stalwarts of the workforce. Their satisfaction comes from maintaining the status quo, making sure things work, services are rendered, and business goes on. There is a need for all types in the workforce of today. The value of information derived from instruments like the Strong Interest Inventory is that people will be able to settle themselves into more satisfying work and derive greater amounts of value from the work they do and be more productive in the process.

Visualizing Your Dream Job
Putting Fantasy to Work

Another way to hone in on your passions is to visualize yourself in a new career. Concentrate on how it would be different from your current one.

** To more clearly establish Jonathan's focus, we began talking about the actual work functions he saw himself doing.*
*"Without any restrictions, without any basis in reality, give me what you think you'd want to do as a career," I challenged him. "You say you want excitement, you want a lifestyle change. What is it you think would be interesting to you?" This exercise was extremely difficult for Jonathan. He found himself unable to relax and open his mind up to creative thinking. **

If you're having trouble with this, try keying in on the hours of the day. It's now eight o'clock in the morning. What are you doing? How is your day progressing? What are you involved with? What's happening around you? How are you dressed? What kind of work environment are you in? What kind of work functions are you involved with? Do people come and ask you questions? What are you responsible for? Are you talking on the telephone? Are you in front of a computer? Describe what you see. What kind of industry do you see yourself in?

** One of Jonathan's major complaints was the predictability of his present job. Getting up, going to work at eight, and coming home at five, like clockwork, if you will. Now he saw himself still asleep at eight o'clock in the morning. He pictured himself waking up between ten and eleven and futzing around his*

30

condo, combining his household regimen with phone calls and other work-related activities, his trusty laptop ever by his side.

"I am sick to death of my routine. I want to work where you sometimes have to stay until three or four in the morning, where there are deadlines and pressures and lots of people running around and you're wondering whether you're going to meet those deadlines. And somehow I picture myself as this little satellite of calm amidst all this, doing my job and doing it well, but having all this activity going on around me. Right now, I'm more interested in a lifestyle change than in making a lot of money. I can afford an entry-level salary for a while, and I can always go back to being an actuary if I want to."

We began to work further with this fantasy. "What kind of industry do you see yourself in?" I asked him. He again pictured this chaos as someplace like a recording studio, or a place where music was produced, possibly music videos. He saw lots of young, energetic entertainers. I asked Jonathan to begin to explore some of the occupations found within the music industry.

He was reticent.

"How could I possibly earn a living in the music field when I'm not interested in being a musician myself? I understand it. I have a great deal of love for music. I play the guitar quite well, but I am not good enough to be a performance artist," he insisted. *

When you have dredged up all you possibly can from this exercise, consider the variety of occupations that industry requires. I asked Jonathan to do a Google search on "Careers in the Music Industry" and see what he came up with. I also asked him to do a book search on www.amazon.com and find out what kind of popular works had been written on the subject of careers in the music industry. Search out people in these occupations, and find out what they do and what it takes to do their jobs. How do people break into this field? What education and experience will you need? Informational interviews are one of the most valuable ways of seeking career information. It not only provides you an opportunity to meet people in the areas of your interests, it has one more important side benefit. You begin to integrate yourself into this new environment. By talking the language, asking pertinent questions, and gaining knowledge, you are beginning to take on the trappings of your new Professional Self without even knowing it. You are in the process of "becoming" who you want to be.

One of the first tasks I assigned Jonathan was to look into different organizations or kinds of businesses within the recording industry, as you will learn to do in Chapter 6. He was surprised with the results. On the list he gave me, organized under three different aspects of the recording industry, were names of people who produced records, talent agents who represented background singers and attorneys who specialized in entertainment law. His list was based solely on what he found interesting and worth looking at. If you had similar interests as Jonathan I suspect your list of interesting organizations would look a lot different based on individual preference..

His next task was to learn about the culture of the industry. The letter requesting an informational interview you see in Chapter 7 resulted from his initial investigation. He now needed to sit down and talk to these people about what was involved. What were recording artists really like in the way they approached life's challenges? What are the day-to-day operations of a person who is a singer in a band? How are club dates made? How are recording contracts drawn up? How do you find backup singers? Who finds dancers to perform in your music videos? What's involved in the production of a compact disc? He needed to know all this and more if he was to figure out where his niche was.

Out of fifteen query letters he sent out, three responded, and Jonathan began to exhibit an excitement I hadn't seen before. Although the thought of making appointments for these gave him goose bumps, he wanted the information, and once they were scheduled, he eagerly anticipated the meetings. He met with an entertainment lawyer, a talent agent, and a producer at Columbia Records. These three people each gave him the names of one or two others who did something a little bit different but were still involved in the industry. Jonathan began to realize it was indeed possible to use his organizational and analytical skills in the music industry.

One of the areas he found attractive was that of personal manager to a recording artist. This seemed to dovetail with the skills that made him a successful actuary: organization, attention to detail, and the ability to work on a variety of projects simultaneously.

"I see myself as the person who makes sure the hotel reservations are made, who gets the airline tickets, who makes sure the hotel has the proper diet and whatever else the artist needs and wants. I see myself as the one who makes sure the stage is set up properly." He saw himself keeping the artist's life uncluttered and free to concentrate on the creative demands of his profession. I watched Jonathan's excitement grow.

He began to see that he could take his lifelong interest in music and apply his technical skills in math and his organizational talents that came from his own self-management skills and involve himself in a very exciting industry that would give him the livelier lifestyle he craved.

"What if this doesn't meet your needs?" I asked Jonathan.

"If it doesn't, I'll look at some of the other areas I've discovered. I never thought I could be involved in any of these simply because I was so focused on performance. Now I have a better appreciation of how many people it takes to bring that performance about. I know I can be one of them, even if I don't know exactly what that is right now."

It took the better part of a year before Jonathan made his change. One of the entertainment lawyers he had interviewed months earlier contacted him about an opening he'd heard about as personal manager for a rising rhythm and blues singer. Jonathan followed up and got the job as the "set up" man, the one who made sure everything was in order for each club date. He traveled extensively, and when he wasn't on the road, he conducted his business from his home. Last I heard, the first album was climbing the charts, and it included one of Jonathan's original compositions. *

Another valuable way to gather information is to look at your past experiences. Everything! Make lists of your high school and collegiate experiences; what clubs did you belong to, where did you volunteer your time, what speakers and lectures were you drawn to, how did you spend your precious free time? All of these are grist for the mill. Most college curricula require a certain amount of exploration during your undergraduate years that falls under titles like general electives. This provides built-in opportunities to explore other majors and academic disciplines in your freshman and sophomore years in order to give you the maximum amount of time to change your mind if you find something that captures your fancy more than your current area of study. Part of the collegiate experience is to explore some of your interests. Many of your interests will be explored primarily outside the classroom. Take a good look at your list of activities; do you start to see anything emerge? Are their characteristics of your list of activities that are similar? Are there persistent themes that emerge as you explore what has interested you in the past? If you are interested in it, it probably won't feel like work. So why not consider some of your areas of interest as a means to employment?

Your clearly defined interests often lead the way for some calculated risk-taking throughout the course of your working life. Your interests will change—what may seem paramount in one stage of your life might become trivial at another time in your life.

I had a student who was studying to be an accountant, and every time she came to class that particular fall quarter her attention was on the earphone attached to what I was to learn was the World Series. She was a baseball fan of the first order, and her team was in the series! She could quote RBI stats, errors made, and the batting averages of more baseball players than I will ever care to know. I asked her if she had thought about working in baseball. She laughed and said, "Oh yeah, I can see me now; working for the Yankees." Well, maybe not for the Yankees, but baseball, like anything else, is a business and business needs accountants. Slowly but surely, she started believing it was possible to work as an accountant in baseball. She researched all the major league baseball parks and teams on the west coast. She looked up the employment section on their various web pages and started applying for accounting jobs in baseball. She went on six interviews over a five-week period and was offered two positions. She accepted a position with QUALCOMM Jack Murphy Stadium in San Diego as her first assignment and has since moved throughout the major baseball leagues, using her knowledge of accounting to work in an area of high interest to her, baseball.

34

As you gather more information, you, too, will realize it is indeed possible to use the skills and experience you have, or are willing to get, in the fields of your passion and interests.

Resources:
Do a Google search under Career Interest Inventories

Personality/Interest Inventory

Circle the numbers of statements that clearly feel like something you might say or do or think—something that feels like you.

1. It's important for me to have a strong, agile body.
2. I need to understand things thoroughly.
3. Music, color, or beauty of any kind can really affect my moods.
4. People enrich my life and give it meaning.
5. I have confidence in myself that I can make things happen.
6. I appreciate clear directions so I know exactly what to do.
7. I can usually carry/build/fix things myself.
8. I can get absorbed for hours in thinking something out.
9. I appreciate beautiful surroundings; color and design mean a lot to me.
10. I love company.
11. I enjoy competing.
12. I need to get my surroundings in order before I start a project.
13. I enjoy making things with my hands.
14. It's satisfying to explore new ideas.
15. I always seem to be looking for new ways to express my creativity.
16. I value being able to share personal concerns with people.
17. Being a key person in a group is very satisfying to me.
18. I take pride in being very careful about all the details of my work.
19. I don't mind getting my hands dirty.
20. I see education as a lifelong process of developing and sharpening my mind.
21. I love to dress in unusual ways, to try new colors and styles.
22. I can often sense when a person needs to talk to someone.
23. I enjoy getting people organized and on the move.
24. A good routine helps me get the job done.
25. I like to buy sensible things that I can make or work on myself.
26. Sometimes I can sit for long periods of time and work on puzzles or read or just think about life.

27. I have a great imagination.
28. It makes me feel good to take care of people.
29. I like to have people rely on me to get the job done.
30. I'm satisfied knowing that I've done an assignment carefully and completely.
31. I'd rather be on my own doing practical, hands-on activities.
32. I'm eager to read about any subject that arouses my curiosity.
33. I love to try creative new ideas.
34. If I have a problem with someone, I prefer to talk it out and resolve it.
35. To be successful, it's important to aim high.
36. I prefer being in a position where I don't have to take responsibility for decisions.
37. I don't enjoy spending a lot of time discussing things. What's right is right.
38. I need to analyze a problem pretty thoroughly before I act on it.
39. I like to rearrange my surroundings to make them unique and different.
40. When I feel down, I find a friend to talk to.
41. After I suggest a plan, I prefer to let others take care of the details.
42. I'm usually content where I am.
43. It's invigorating to do things outdoors.
44. I keep asking "why?"
45. I like my work to be an expression of my moods and feelings.
46. I like to find ways to help people care more for each other.
47. It's exciting to take part in important decisions.
48. I'm always glad to have someone else take charge.
49. I like my surroundings to be plain and practical.
50. I need to stay with a problem until I figure out an answer.
51. The beauty of nature touches something deep inside me.
52. Close relationships are important to me.
53. Promotion and advancement are important to me.
54. Efficiency, for me, means doing a set amount carefully each day.

55. A strong system of law and order is important to prevent chaos.
56. Thought-provoking books always broaden my perspective.
57. I look forward to seeing art shows, plays, and good films.
58. When I haven't seen a person for a long time, I'd love to know how he or she is doing.
59. It's exciting to influence people.
60. When I say I'll do it, I follow through on every detail.
61. Good, hard, physical work never hurt anyone.
62. I'd like to learn all there is to know about subjects that interest me.
63. I don't want to be like everyone else; I like to do things differently.
64. I often want people to tell me how I can help them.
65. I'm willing to take some risks to get ahead.
66. I like exact directions and clear rules when I start something new.
67. The first thing I look for in a car is a well-built engine.
68. I often think, "These people are intellectually stimulating."
69. When I'm creating, I tend to let everything else go.
70. I feel concerned that so many people in our society need help.
71. It's fun to get ideas across to people.
72. I hate it when they keep changing the system just when I get it down.
73. I usually know how to take care of things in an emergency.
74. Just reading about new discoveries is exciting.
75. I like to create happenings.
76. I often go out of my way to pay attention to people who seem lonely and friendless.
77. I love a bargain.
78. I don't like to do things unless I'm sure they're approved.
79. Sports are important in building strong bodies.
80. I've always been curious about the way nature works.
81. It's fun to be in a mood to try or do something unusual.
82. I believe that people are basically good.
83. If I don't make it the first time, I usually bounce back with energy and enthusiasm.
84. I appreciate knowing exactly what people expect of me.

85. I like to take things apart to see if I can fix them.
86. My attitude is: "Don't get excited. We can think it out and plan the right move logically."
87. It would be hard to imagine my life without beauty around me.
88. People often seem to tell me their problems.
89. I can usually connect with people who get me in touch with a network of resources.
90. I don't need much to be happy.

Scoring Your Answers

To score, circle the same numbers below that you circled on the preceding pages.

R	I	A	S	E	C
1	2	3	4	5	6
7	8	9	10	11	12
13	14	15	16	17	18
19	20	21	22	23	24
25	26	27	28	29	30
31	32	33	34	35	36
37	38	39	40	41	42
43	44	45	46	47	48
49	50	51	52	53	54
55	56	57	58	59	60
61	62	63	64	65	66
67	68	69	70	71	72
73	74	75	76	77	78
79	80	81	82	83	84
85	86	87	88	89	90

Now add up the number of circles in each column:

R____   I____   A____   S____   E____   C____

Which are your three highest scores:

1st _____   2nd _____   3rd _____

Source

From: Michelozzi, Betty Neville. *Coming Alive from Nine to Five*. Mayfield, 1996, 1992, 1988, 1984, 1980, Corralitos, Ca.

Holland's Occupational Themes
Typical Characteristics

Realistic: Practical and active, with good physical skills. Someone who enjoys working outside and creating things with his or her hands. Prefers to deal with things rather than ideas or people. Sometimes has difficulty expressing ideas in words or communicating feelings to others. Political and economic ideas are fairly conventional.

Typical occupations:
Athletic trainer
Forester
Radiology technician
Police officer
Military services
Electrician
Architect
Engineer
Carpenter

Investigative: Prefers to solve abstract problems and understands the physical world rather than acting upon the world. Enjoys complicated problems and intellectual challenges. Tends not to like structured situations, lots of rules, or working around many people.

Typical occupations:
Computer programmer
Medical professions
Chemist
Pharmacist
Psychologist
Police officer
Mathematician
Science teacher
Systems analyst

Artistic: Prefers unstructured situations where problems are dealt with through self-expression in the artistic media. Prefers to work alone, has a great need for individualistic expression, and is sensitive and emotional. Would describe self as independent, original, unconventional, expressive, and energetic.

Typical occupations:
Art teacher
Interior decorator
Photographer
Cosmetologist
Reporter
Public relations director
Advertising
English teacher

Social: Sociable, responsible, humanistic, and concerned with the welfare of others. Expresses self well and gets along well with others. Likes to be near the center of groups and prefers to solve problems by discussing them with others. Sees self as cheerful, popular, achieving, and possessing good leadership skills.

Typical occupations:
Public school administrator
Guidance counselor
Recreation leader
Social worker
Occupational therapist
Speech pathologist
Elementary school teacher

Enterprising: Has great facility with words and puts them to effective use in selling and leading. Enjoys persuading others to his or her viewpoint and is impatient with work involving precision or long periods of intellectual concentration. Sees self as energetic, enthusiastic, adventurous, self-confident, and dominant.

Typical occupations:
Restaurant manager
Travel agent
Buyer
Marketing executive
Personnel director
Investment manager
Store manager
Realtor
Dental hygienist

Conventional: Prefers highly ordered activities, does not like to be a leader, and likes working in a well-established chain of command. Likes to know exactly what is expected of him or her, and feels uncomfortable when he or she doesn't know the "rules." Sees self as conventional, stable, well controlled, and dependable.

Typical occupations:
Accountant
Banker
Secretary
Credit manager
Dietician
Dental assistant
Business education teacher

3   Identifying Your Skills
Don't Overlook the Obvious

"Until you begin to look at the skills you have and how they empower you, you may find it difficult to believe in yourself."

In my work with clients, I am constantly bombarded by remarks ranging from "I have nothing to offer an employer; I have no skills" to "All I know how to do is this one job. How can I possibly change careers if this is all I know how to do?" Or another variation on the theme is something like, "Oh I know I'm a skilled individual, but I just can't tell you what those skills are." College graduates come in terrified that their research institutions have only taught them how to be researchers, college professors, or good students. Some students will come in perplexed about what they can do. Some will say things like, "I know a lot of things, and I know a lot about things, but I'm not sure of what I can do with all this information." It's almost as if they wish to categorize accomplishments as irrelevant before a potential employer has the chance to do it for them. Many of us go through life wearing these blinders. Thirty percent of college students strongly believe their first *job* defines their *career*, according to Phil Gardner, Collegiate Employment Research Institute.

To make my point, try this. Look at the following sentence.

> *"Feature films are the result of years of scientific study combined with the experience of years."*

How many **f**'s are there in the statement? Do you see two? Three? Five? No cheating. Did you come up with six? If you didn't, go back and see if you can find them all now.

As you can see, all too often we overlook the obvious. As you begin your own personal assessment, you may run into the same problem. Overlooking the obvious. It's time to throw away your blinders.

Employers will judge experiences according to their own criteria. Your job is to show how the skills and experiences you already have prepare you for this position, to sell yourself as a

47

qualified person for this particular opening. Defining those skills is a challenging venture.

Pat Erickson was a good example of that.

"I need help in writing a résumé," she announced upon entering my office.

"Why is that?" I asked, waving her to a chair.

"I've applied for a promotion to assistant buyer."

I nodded.

"No, you don't understand," she insisted. "I have to get this job. I can't just apply for it; I must get this job."

I asked for some background.

Until the age of forty, she had been a career wife and mother. During her twenty-year marriage, she had successfully raised two children and was well known for her community involvement. Her husband, Ted, a union laborer working in the mining industry, made good money, but they had worked hard to raise a family on just one salary. Both valued Pat's involvement in their children's education and in the community, and by careful management, they had built up a modest savings.

"The trouble started in the summer of 2000," she explained. Hard times hit the mining industry in which Ted had spent his working life. The company announced layoffs.

"We weren't particularly concerned in the beginning. This had happened before. We would just wait out this storm as we had the others."

Only this time was different. The layoff lasted three and a half years.

At the end of the first year, the Ericksons faced the fact that Ted could not rely on being rehired in the foreseeable future.

"That's when I began thinking about going to work." It was frightening. The mine was the major employer in the community, and the layoffs affected the entire job market. There were few jobs, period. Pat was also uncertain about what she was capable of doing because she had never worked for a paycheck.

"I'd never done anything," she told me. "I'd never supported anyone; I'd never worked for anyone."

In desperation, Pat applied for and got a job at a tortilla factory located about five miles from her home, as an ordinary

48

*laborer on the assembly line at minimum wage. Although the
tortilla factory was still a family owned and operated enterprise, it
was a large company, employing hundreds of people in an industry
grossing in the millions of dollars annually.*

*"I learned the job in the first week, met my quotas the
second, and was bored by the third," she recalled. Although her
creative mind rebelled against the tediousness of the work, she
recognized it for what it was—a job, and her family desperately
needed the income.*

*"But it wasn't long before I realized minimum wage wasn't
enough to support my family." Something had to be done.*

*As she patiently fed tortillas into the oven, she pondered the
problem. She liked the company, felt comfortable there, she
admitted, and determined that it was a new position, not a new
company she needed. Her enterprising intellect began cataloging
the other jobs around her, and she began to think about what else
she could do. She felt uncomfortable about her lack of experience,
but she needed to make more money. Necessity, the mother of all
motivators, pushed her to look more aggressively at what might be
available. **

According to Richard Bolles, author of the legendary *What
Color Is Your Parachute*, the average college graduate has at his
disposal a range of between 800 and 2,000 potentially marketable
skills. As we gain work and life experiences, our "skills bank"
should increasing accordingly. In developing a career plan for
yourself, you must be able to recognize the skills you have already
mastered from all aspects of your life.

Start by understanding that there are different kinds of skills,
and some of them are not always acquired through education or
training. Sometimes skills are natural tendencies or personality
traits, sometimes they are skills you developed through hobbies
and interests, and sometimes they are job-related skills. These
skills are yours to do with as you wish. You can store them away
to be used at a later date, or you can use them every day.

* *"Last week I noticed an open position as an assistant
buyer. I figured all my life I've been buying things, and on a very*

restrictive budget," she told me. "It was payday. I looked at my check and made the decision to apply."

The job was on a paraprofessional level and required a résumé. She had never done this. That's when she came to see me.

"Why do you feel you're qualified to be an assistant buyer?" I asked.

"Because all my life I've bought things," she reiterated. "Up until now, Ted's always made good money, but we've only had one income and so I had to be quite frugal in my purchases. The position calls for a buying assistant. I would just be buying different things in greater quantity."

*I pointed out that her reasoning was somewhat naïve. I could see her confidence deflate, but just for an instant. She straightened herself up in the chair, set her jaw, and said again, "I need this job." ***

There are three commonly accepted categories of skills, loosely defined as:

***Transferable skills,* which can be transferred to and implemented in many different interest areas and work settings.** These "soft skills" are mainly acquired through experience rather than formal training. They are less easy to recognize because they tend to be linked to dealing with processes rather than doing things. Some samples are given at the end of the chapter. Do keep in mind that transferable skills will not substitute for technical skills.

They include: thinking critically, analyzing, listening, presentation, creativity, mathematical ability, computer ease, goal setting, teamwork, design, delegating, negotiating, influencing, coaching, motivating, information gathering, budgeting, writing, management, interviewing, observation, researching, organizing, problem solving, decision making, language ability, leadership, teaching, time management, debating, setting priorities, troubleshooting, promoting, scheduling, adaptability, communicating, coordinating, and selling.

The ten hottest transferable skills, according to noted career-change counselor Howard Figler, Ph.D., are budget management, supervising, public relations, coping with deadline pressures, negotiating/arbitrating, speaking, writing, interviewing, organizing/managing/coordinating, and teaching/instructing.

***Technical/work knowledge skills,* which reflect your ability to perform the tasks associated with a specific occupation or profession.** These "hard skills" are easy to recognize because they are often identified as "qualifications" for specific jobs. These skills tend to be associated with specific tasks or job functions and are often harder to transfer from one field to another.

They include: laboratory functions and techniques, software/hardware knowledge, public relations, accounting, interior design, social research, waste management, word processing, policy analysis, field testing, commercial banking, newsletter writing, systems architecture, telemarketing, benefits/compensation, translation, nursing, medicine, electrical, engineering, drafting, graphic design, advertising, web design, and marketing research.

***Personal management skills,* which reflect your ability to get along smoothly with others in work settings and to manage different stresses on the job as well as in other areas of your life.** According to the National Association of Colleges and Employers (NACE), the number one reason college graduates are discharged from their first job is their inability to work and get along with their co-workers.

They include: warmth, sensitivity, drive, humor, self-confidence, sincerity, honesty, respect for diversity, risk-taking, responsibility, assertiveness, attention to detail, integrity, energy, determination, accountability, inner strength, enthusiasm, thoughtfulness, vision, depth, ethics, loyalty, cooperation, maturity, intelligence, global thinking, optimism.

The National Association of Colleges and Employers recently identified twelve skills that will be needed to be a success in the future. It is not necessary to have all of them, but a combination of them throughout your life will provide stability and opportunities in a variety of areas. These skills are:

1. Flexibility and adaptability to handle ever-changing roles and management.
2. Diversity in ability to function and work with people from a broad range of cultures and learning styles.
3. Language skills—especially knowledge of multiple languages for the global marketplace.
4. Computer literacy and basic knowledge in all types of technology.
5. Team players. Negotiating and networking skills a must.
6. Learning skills and continuous reeducation. We all must be lifelong learners.
7. Personal career planning skills. Ability to forecast and accommodate career change.
8. Global awareness/orientation. Knowledge of a country and region as well as of the people there.
9. Oral and written communications skills become even more valuable as corporations flatten. People must be self-starters.
10. Self-comfort. The company no longer defines the worker.
11. Strong ethical framework.
12. Forecasting skills, knowing where your company is going, where the opportunities are, and the ability to see which direction to flex toward.

It is important to note that this list describes areas of character, ethics, and individual discipline much more than actual technical skills. The need for strong moral fiber will continue to play a significant role in our collective well-being as we move forward in the twenty-first century.

Communicating Your Assets
Developing a Skills Vocabulary

Your first step is to develop a vocabulary for describing skills in general. One of the most difficult parts of the job search is the development of this professional vocabulary. We are in the process of identifying your Professional Self, and to take it on the road and put it to work, we need a way to describe what we have and what we bring to the job market. Developing this career vocabulary will go a long way in starting to develop the self-confidence you need in order to conduct a successful job search. Being able to talk about yourself in positive, life-affirming ways that are grounded in your life experiences creates the most concrete foundation for the beginnings of your Professional Self. In order get a handle on it, take a blank sheet of paper and a pencil and write down all twenty-six letters of the alphabet on the left-hand side of the page. Take three minutes. As quickly as you can, write down an adjective or action verb that begins with each of the letters of the alphabet. This exercise stimulates your brain to think of words to help you articulate your skills. These words also are essential later as you prepare your résumé and get ready for interviews.

You may get stuck at first, but keep trying. Remember that you are in the process of learning a new skill, and it will feel awkward at first. Anytime we try something new, there is a period of adjustment. Learning how to do a good skills assessment takes practice, and the expansion of your vocabulary is not an easy thing to do either, so give yourself a little time with this. Take a look at the lists above in the transferable, technical, and personal management section; use them as a guide. Get yourself a thesaurus. This does not have to be hard. It just has to be done. Remember, psychologists say it takes twelve weeks of daily reinforcement for anything to be incorporated into our repertoire of responses. So if you are a little frustrated by your lack of vocabulary as you do this exercise, give yourself a break; you are learning something new. The exciting thing is that when you learn to identify your skills you will then learn to use that information in a whole new way. That's the fun part and another chapter.

But back to the task at hand....

Here's a sample of the kinds of words you might think about and begin to incorporate into your own career mind-set:

A .....Adapted
B .....Budgeted
C .....Communicated
D .....Developed
E .....Evaluated
F .....Filed
G .....Generated
H .....Hired
I ..... Investigated
J ..... Juggled, judged, just,
K .....Kept
L .....Lead
M .....Managed
N .....Negotiated
O .....Operated
P .....Persuaded
Q .....Qualified
R .....Researched
S .....Supervised
T .....Translated
U .....Utilized
V .....Verbalized
W .....Wrote
X .....Xeroxed
Y .....Yield
Z .....Zany

Make a new list every day for a week. By the end of the week, you should be able to comfortably list words for at least twenty-four out of the twenty-six letters. I'll give you a break with x and z, and you might have a little difficulty with k, j, and q, too. The rest should begin to come more easily with practice. Try to come up with different words every day; do this exercise, and be sure to keep your lists. Now apply those words to your own life experience. Learn not to trivialize your assets, but think about contexts in which they have been useful. Then break them down into functional, technical, and personal management skills.

"I don't have time for this," Pat objected.

"Yes, you do. The job doesn't close for two more weeks. When you bring these back, you'll be amazed at what we will have to work with."

Equipped with her seven lists of words, Pat returned the next week.

*On three separate sheets of paper, Pat broke down her skills into each of the skill areas. Some did not fit exactly into any of the categories, but I asked her to pick the one that came closest. ***

This kind of self-assessment is often revealing. Think of it as creating a shopping list of your assets: your interests, learned skills, natural aptitudes, and work-related achievements and experiences; something you can do as well as, or better than, most people. It isn't easy. It takes dedicated practice. Begin by focusing on your successes and achievements and what brought them about, and it will get easier as you go along.

There is an extra benefit to this exercise. The process of skills identification and developing a skills inventory involves the issue of choice, giving you the power to decide which skills you will use on your new job. If you decide that a skill you have mastered is one you don't want to use on your next job, it's your choice not to include it. Just because you are very good at something doesn't mean that you have to use it in your next job. I was told a story early in my career by another social worker friend who mentioned he was often being urged by his bosses to move "up the ladder," as it were. They thought he would be a natural for administration, and twelve years in the military as an NCO had told my friend Jesse that he had had enough of administration in his life. He was a practitioner; he wanted to see clients, and he loved his job working with adults living with mental illness. "Just because everybody, including you, thinks you would be good at something doesn't mean you have to do it. If it's not the right fit, regardless of how good you are at it, you are going to feel trapped in the long run." That statement has freed me several times to turn down administrative positions, to my own benefit and to the benefit of the organizations offering me the opportunity! Really knowing what skills you have that you value most gives you an tremendous amount of power in picking job responsibilities because you can get your job description right down to the essence of your skill set and really be able to work at your full potential. How exciting is that!

Search through your work and education history. Select out of that bag what you want to carry to your next job, those to bank for future use, those you will have to acquire to achieve the level of employment you're seeking, and those to leave behind. The choice is yours.

For instance, the secretary who can assess her true skills may find she is actually doing the work of an office manager and purchasing agent. The teacher who has brought in thousands of dollars in grant money may realize she has skills as a fund-raiser. A loan officer probably has marketing and analytical skills. A volunteer who has done public relations work for her church or women's organization can often transfer those skills to paid employment.

Log On to Your Current Skills
Dissecting Your Past

Another way to develop a skills list is to keep a log of your job duties. Focus on what you do on a daily basis or what you've done in the past. Think about the skills you use to perform each task.

Another way of uncovering your skills is to take a specific experience, one you remember in vivid detail, one you are especially proud of, and one in which you played an active role. This can be something you did while working, something you achieved through involvement with community or social groups, or maybe something that improved your family's home life. Focus on those things that are of paramount importance to the employer—those activities and accomplishments that the employer perceives to be important to the organization's long-term strategic goals.

Employers also want to know about leadership, taking responsibility for a project, setting a goal, and bringing together the people and resources to achieve that goal.

* Thinking back over her career as a mother, job description firmly in had as she reviewed the qualifications; Pat identified her PTA involvement as her most significant experience.

Although she had held leadership positions throughout the years, her most spectacular accomplishment came with her first dive into the water. When her children were in the second and third grades, she realized they needed help in developing their reading skills. Too bad there were no reading labs in the schools, the teachers told her. A private tutor was beyond her means. Believing there were other families in the same predicament, she brought this up at the next PTA meeting. As organizations of this kind are wont to do, she was told, "If this is important to you, why don't you take the ball and run with it?"

Accepting the challenge, she recruited three other mothers whose children also had reading difficulties, and together they approached the school board at one of its regularly scheduled meetings and asked why there were no reading labs. The board was sympathetic to their concerns, but pointed out it had been unable to get these labs funded. Pat asked what needed to be done and was told a grant proposal needed to be written to thoroughly document the need with supporting material, including a budget, program development and implementation, control systems, and evaluation of results. It sounded overwhelming, and I'm sure the board never expected to hear from Pat or her committee again.

Nevertheless, the creation of the reading labs was important, so Pat broke the project down into specific tasks and assigned one to each of the women on her committee. One was to learn the process for writing a grant. She assigned another to collect the documentation of need by contacting other parents whose children were in the same age group. The other was to gather signatures for support of the reading labs. Pat took on the budget preparation. All these were bite-sized pieces that each worked on individually over the next few months. They met weekly to discuss their progress.

As the project began to take more shape and purpose, Pat began to see the need for expert advice.

She recontacted the superintendent's office to ask for information and assistance. She found she got better response when she put her requests in writing. I pointed out that this required communication skills. She was getting her needs across to other people who in turn were answering her requests. She was also making sure that there was communication all up and down the line, from the school board to the PTA to her and her committee.

When it came time to present the findings to the school board, the group appointed her to make the presentation. By using charts and graphs made at her kitchen table, she clearly documented the need, presented a budget that seemed workable, and talked about alternative budgets in terms of cost-saving measures. She kept the presentation to just under an hour and provided enough convincing material that the project received the necessary approval for proposal development. A professional grant writer, employed by the school district, was assigned to work with the women on the formal proposal, which was also approved and funded. The final grant affected not just Pat's school and her children, but the entire district. *

Don't overlook your volunteer experience. Look at your unpaid efforts as meaningful work experience. Employers will pay attention to these activities, but only if you are capable of articulating their significance to the position at hand. They are especially interested if you prepared a budget, edited or wrote a newsletter, designed advertising flyers, held office, organized conferences and other meetings, or raised funds, but you must be able to articulate their significance to the position. For instance, Ana Delgado was a flight attendant who sought and won a corporate communications job. One of the reasons she could make this transition was that she had produced newsletters while she was a flight supervisor. She also was considered to have labor-relations experience because she had been her fellow flight attendants' union representative—also an unpaid job. Through working with Ana to identify her skill sets, she dismissed at first the very two things the employers said gave her the upper hand and got her the job. Her knowledge of production and design of print material, because of her work on the newsletter, was something the committee had been looking for. Anne had used her public speaking skills when she was called upon to draft and issue press releases during union negotiations that averted a strike, saving the airline lost revenue and reputation with the consumer. With these two examples alone, she had beat out the competition. Do not overlook the obvious. Another thing to remember is that you never know what the employer is looking for. In this case, Ana's particular choice of skill sets to focus on in the interview is what proved to be the deciding factor for her employer.

Realize that often the things that are most important to us are the things we learn from the most and have the best chance at a professional payoff. One example is Catherine Chen, a former junior high school art teacher, who volunteered for fund-raising projects and assisted participants at a therapeutic riding facility for the handicapped where her son was enrolled. The center's assistant director recognized her commitment and eventually encouraged her to apply for the full-time, paid position of volunteer coordinator. This position would allow her to continue to retain her teaching credential and more importantly to be on campus with her son, who would now receive a scholarship as a staff child. In this position, she was responsible for recruiting, hiring, and training a staff of 200 volunteers, writing press releases, and handling all of the center's publicity.

"Volunteering was a good way for me to learn a new business because of the hands-on training," she says. "And even though I didn't earn a salary, it definitely paid off down the road. This new position allows me to keep my teaching credential current, and I received a nice raise and new title. The best perk to the job is that my son and I are able to see each other several times a day while still living independent lives."

Try writing down your most memorable experience. Describe your part in it. It may take you several paragraphs or two or three pages, depending on the degree of detail you recall from the experience. Don't rush. Linger over the memory. Is there anything else that needs to be recalled?

Responsibilities + Skills = Accomplishments
Add Meaning to Your Skills

Once you are comfortable that you have remembered as much as you can of this experience, take your script and use the action verbs, adjectives, and descriptors you developed to articulate it in terms of the skills required.

If you have been a student or career wife and mother, you'll draw most heavily on your volunteer skills, academic experience and internships, and leadership positions in clubs and organizations. If you have formal work experience, you want to categorize the skills you're now using or have acquired in past positions. Describe in detail your duties. Next, begin to attach skills to those duties, and then think about the accomplishments of the activity. For each activity you dissect, ask yourself:

- What did the activity involve? (Responsibilities)
- What did it take to accomplish those responsibilities? (Skills)
- What was the result? (Accomplishments)

This will enable you to describe your skills in concise, unambiguous terms; back up your claims by referring to actual experiences in your life, and make a clear connection between your skills and the needs of the employer.

* We began with a hard look at Pat's job description. The major duty was to assist the buyer in the requisitioning and purchasing of staples for the tortillas, but the job required several additional skills: organization skills, some writing, and communication and accounting skills.

As we began to explore and identify the skills she possessed, her confidence resurfaced.

I pointed out that she acted in a supervisory capacity because she controlled the reading labs project. She took responsibility for it, and she segregated and delegated the tasks that needed to be done. Making sure that each member of her team stayed on track was again a management responsibility. She also provided the necessary nurturing and encouragement that kept them willing and able to work on the project. She had used creative and analytical skills when she conceived ways to get the required materials, components, and services in a cost-effective manner. She had negotiated prices, terms, and schedules with vendors to develop the budget she submitted, a key skill for the job she was now after. She had used oral communication in delivering her presentation and written communication in clarifying the information she needed to make the initial presentation and then the formal grant proposal. And most important, the results of Pat's efforts were documented.

Pat could now see that her PTA experience had given her budgeting experience, communication skills, supervisory skills, management skills, and the ability to keep people on track and working toward the same goal, all of which correlated to the qualifications outlined in the job description for the assistant buyer. Pat was able to take what she saw as a basically "homemaker" situation and turn it into an experience that clearly demonstrated the kinds of skills required by the job she was after. She was able to break her skills down by the components required for the new position. She was able to tell her employers that she had developed the requirements of the job over a long period of time, and that she used these skills on a consistent basis. What she had done could be effectively put to work in planning and securing large-scale purchases and working effectively with vendors to meet the needs of her company. They believed her and offered her the job. *

Until you begin to look at the skills you have and how they empower you, you may also find it difficult to believe in yourself as worthy of the confidence you want your new employer to place in you. By getting to know the skills you already have in hand, you can use this confidence to take a greater degree of control over your career search.

* After seven months, her supervisor was promoted to another position, and Pat was again interviewed. Based primarily on her performance and her ability to articulate the new skills she had acquired, management offered her the buyer's position. She continued to grow with the company and to develop and apply

more skills. The last time I saw her, she was so excited she could hardly wait to get the social preliminaries out of the way.

"You'll never guess what," she blurted immediately. "My Business and Professional Women's chapter just named me 'Woman of the Year!'" *

Constant practice of this process will make it routine. The operative word is "practice." With practice and reinforcement, I guarantee the results will improve your self-esteem and give you a better understanding of your Professional Self. Developing this Career Vocabulary will go a long way in the job market. It will help you develop strong résumés and relevant examples of your work experience and its relationship to the job at hand. When it comes time to negotiate, you will have good, solid evidence of what it takes to get those signing bonuses, tuition credits, student loan repayment programs, and so forth. This is a very important step in the process. It will provide so much information we will use in so many ways throughout the rest of the steps of the Professional Self Model. Another thing that happens as a result of a good skills assessment is that you begin to believe in your self in a different way. You see yourself emerging into a new self-concept that will take you to work and back. It is very empowering to begin to feel the potential of your Professional Self. Get started now. You will discover a new you hiding behind the obvious.

Skill Classification

Below is a sample of skills and their applications based on the work of Paul Breen and Urban Whitaker in consultation with students, faculty members, and employers in the humanities and behavioral and social sciences. As you identify your skills, think of the situations where you used them, and what resulted.

Information Management Skills involve the ability to:
> Sort data and objects.
> Apply information creatively to specific problems or tasks.
> Understand and use organizing principles.
> Evaluate information against appropriate standards.
> Synthesize facts, concepts, and principles.

Valuing Skills involve the ability to:
> Assess a course of action in terms of its long-range effects on general human welfare.
> Make decisions that will maximize both individual and collective good.

Communication Skills involve the ability to:
> Listen with objectivity and paraphrase the content of a message.
> Use various forms and styles of written communication.
> Speak effectively to individuals and groups.
> Use media formats to present ideas imaginatively.
> Express one's needs, wants, opinions, and preferences without offending the sensitivities of others.

Research and Investigation Skills involve the ability to:
> Identify information sources appropriate to special needs or problems.
> Apply a variety of methods to test the validity of data.
> Identify problems and needs.
> Design an experiment, plan, or model that systematically defines a problem.
> Formulate questions relevant to clarifying a particular problem, topic, or issue.

Critical Thinking Skills involve the ability to:

    Identify quickly and accurately the critical issues when making a decision or solving a problem.

    Identify a general principle that explains the interrelated experiences or factual data.

    Identify reasonable criteria for assessing the value or appropriateness of an action or behavior and apply to strategies and action plans.

    Adapt one's concepts and behavior to changing conventions and norms.

    Create innovative solutions to complex problems.

    Analyze the interrelationships of events and ideas from several perspectives.

Design and Planning Skills involve the ability to:

    Identify alternative courses of action.

    Assess needs and set realistic goals and priorities.

    Follow through with a plan or decision.

    Manage time effectively.

    Predict future trends and patterns.

    Accommodate multiple demands of time, energy, and resources.

Management and Administration Skills involve the ability to:

    Motivate and lead people.

    Identify resource materials useful in the solution of a problem.

    Delegate responsibility for the completion of a task.

Human Relations and Interpersonal Skills involve the ability to:

    Keep a group "on track" and moving toward the achievement of a common goal.

    Use argumentation techniques to persuade others.

    Make commitments to persons.

    Be willing to take risks.

    Teach a skill, concept, or principle to others.

    Work under time and environment pressures.

Personal and Career Development Skills involve the ability to:
> Analyze and learn from life experiences—both one's own and others'.
> Relate the skills developed in one environment to the requirements of another.
> Persist with a project when faced with failure.
> Recognize when a project cannot be carried out or is not worth the effort required to complete it.
> Generate trust and confidence in others.

Adapted from Paul Breen and Urban Whitaker, *The Learning Center* © 1982.

4 Determining Your Work Values
Setting Priorities

"Values are the emotional salary of work."

We usually think of careers as vehicles for achieving material well-being, psychological growth, and personal fulfillment, but as human beings we have additional spiritual and altruistic needs: the desire for a rewarding purpose, the need to be meaningfully related to the rest of humanity, and the desire to use one's talents in the service of others.

Howard Figler, author of the classic *The Complete Job-Search Handbook*, takes this one step further.

"Your selection of one particular kind of work from among the thousands available must reflect what you regard as important, worth doing, inherently valuable." He describes values as the "emotional salary of work." Look at work values as attitudinal measuring sticks for determining your most important sources of satisfaction, be that working with disabled people, dancing, growing plants, involving yourself in social change, making decisions with numbers, selling ideas, working in space, or creating beautiful music.

Dr. Figler goes on to write about four kinds of values to take into consideration when looking at your work. They are:

1. Material values—Will it accommodate and finance my current or desired lifestyle?
2. Social values—Will I enjoy the people I work with and the people I serve? Will I enjoy the companionship as much as the work?
3. Emotional values—Will I enjoy the work itself. Will I look forward to solving the problems this kind of work entails? Will I be able to handle the frustrations?
4. Spiritual values—Will this work contribute to the greater good? This question applies to every line of work. How much would my work be missed if I were not here to do it?

Few positions embrace all dimensions equally, but all four should be part of every job choice. Any dimension that is completely ignored will come back to haunt you. If, for example, you are satisfied by the material, emotional, and spiritual components, but not fulfilled by the social, it will eventually make the job a problem. When what you do is congruent with what you value, you achieve the best form of personal productivity, and your self-esteem soars.

These broad themes are sometimes referred to as "unifying principles," golden nuggets of truth used as a guide for goal planning and living. Today's typical career path is like a series of crossroads. At each junction, you must decide to go in one direction and not another. Change is risky, but risk is the price of admission. Ask yourself: What is there in my life that I value, and what is missing from it? How can I use my working life to address some of the goals and things I would like to have my life be about? How much of a part will work play in my overall identity as an adult? The answers give you direction. Facing up to these questions may be frightening at the outset, but this fear is no reason to delay getting on with it. With all the time and energy you spend at work, being fulfilled from Monday to Friday is a large measure of how happy you are with life in general. I often see people who are successful in their careers but are unhappy because they get no "emotional salary" from their work. You can avoid that.

Begin by identifying your values in relation to how you live your life, how you feel about work, and how you relate to other people. These contribute to your sense of self-worth as much as to a stable career path. An incomplete awareness of your values can lead you to make conflicting choices that you later regret. If the changes you make in your life reflect your deeply felt goals and desires, the natural stress that accompanies them will be minimal and can even be positive.

Your reassessment doesn't have to result in a drastic change of direction. Sometimes a shift in emphasis—maybe incorporating more client contact into your job, or working with a team of people you really respect and enjoy—is all it takes to customize your current position. Other times, a complete career overhaul is needed.

This was Sara Miller's dilemma when a career change was thrust upon her.

In the beginning, it was frightening. The pain, the numbness, the swelling in her hands and arms as her capable fingers manipulated the dental tools was excruciating, and it occurred more and more often. Diagnosis: carpal tunnel syndrome, an ailment common to people who perform repetitive tasks and quick movements with their hands over a period of time. The specialists and the rehabilitation counselor agreed. An operation could relieve her pain, but the ultimate cure was to leave the profession that aggravated the problem.

Cold fear gripped her stomach. Her children depended upon her. Could she afford to change?

Gradually, the panicky feeling subsided, pushed aside as she mulled the possibilities of new challenges, only to surface again as the mortgage payment came due.

"I know I'm capable. I know I have skills. I just don't seem to be able to figure out where a retired dental hygienist takes her chips to find a new game," she told me.

I could understand her concern. Initially, Sara said she wanted her next career to be something that was more prestigious than the last. Her big fear was that she was going to have to sacrifice her income to do that. *

The realities of career change often require an income reduction. You may have a position of responsibility you have worked hard to achieve, which compensates you for that accomplishment. When entering a new field, you will probably start at the bottom. You need to think about how important this is to you. Think about the long term as well. Will you be happy at this job five years from now? And if the difference is too much, that's okay. You haven't burned any bridges or locked yourself into anything yet.

Another reality is that you may need retraining to achieve your highest values. This might mean adding a degree, earning a certificate, qualifying for a license, or gaining experience in the field through internships and training programs.

We briefly discussed Sara's options, among them retraining. She was adamant.

"I'm not interested in going back to school. I don't want to take the time, and I don't have the energy. Besides, I need something right now, not two years down the road." She would have to take her experience and parlay that into a new career. So we moved on from there.

To start with, we looked at what she especially liked about being a dental hygienist.

"First was the money," she acknowledged. "I earned up to $400 a day, depending on the number of bookings I arranged. I made somewhere around $65,000 a year, not bad for a woman without a college degree, is it?" She and her children lived quite comfortably, and she was proud of that.

She had contracted independently with several local dentists and found she liked this flexibility. It allowed her to work around her children's needs and school schedules. She also liked the leisure time this flexibility afforded her.

"I liked the idea of helping others. I liked feeling I made a difference in people's lives."

On the downside was lack of security.

"Look at me right now." As an independent agent, when she was unable to see clients because she was ill, she lost that income.

Because she contracted with five different dentists in town, no one claimed her; there was no sense of loyalty to her, and she missed that.

"It's basically the same kind of function on a day-to-day basis," she complained. This had caused her disability in the first place, the tediousness of the job, the continuousness of the tasks.

She was especially dissatisfied at the lack of prestige she perceived the profession commanded.

"People see dental hygienists as just janitors of the mouth. When the dentist is done with all the technical work that makes the mouth function, then the dental hygienist comes in and does the clean-up work," she said.

"People take for granted what I do," she continued. "There is never any feedback on my performance. Patients don't have any idea of what's going on when their mouths are open and they're staring up into the light. Once you've established yourself, dentists very seldom come in and check your work," she explained. "You have to develop your own sense of positive reinforcement." *

Discovering What You Want
Values Clarification

To help clarify what you want in your next career, complete the values clarification exercise you will find at the end of the chapter. The exercise asks you to rate the importance of each of the following work values on a scale of one to eight, with eight being highest: High Income, Prestige, Independence, Helping Others, Security, Variety, Leadership, Working in Your Main Field of Interest, Leisure, Challenge, Interpersonal Relations, and Creativity. (See the exercise for precise definitions of these values.)

There are two parts to the exercise. You'll need two copies of the Value Scale. For the first part, fill out the first scale in terms of how you feel about your current work. Then do the same in the second column for what you want in your next career.

* Sara took the exercise home with her and returned the next day. She found conflicting responses in the areas of Prestige, Security, Variety, Leadership, Challenge, and Creativity, pinpointing facets she wanted to change. *

When You Can't Have Everything
Looking at Choices

One of the most difficult things for people to accept when launching a new career search is the necessity of compromise. To be happy with the compromises you do make, you must first establish what is really important in your life. Then you can decide what you are willing to give up to achieve that.

To determine which of these values you've just identified command your highest priority and which were really just "nice to have," total your Initial Score column on your second copy of the scale.

The crux of this exercise is to achieve an exact score of forty-eight. If the total exceeds this score, you must go back to each value and adjust or eliminate the original scores so that the total comes down to no more than forty-eight. The adjusted scores are entered in the second column. This "Adjusted Score" then reflects those values about which you feel strongest. (If the total is less than forty-eight, you aren't off the hook. You must adjust and add until you reach the magic number. It's the forced choice that really tests and confirms your values.)

My clients sometimes do this exercise two or three times throughout our sessions together. Each time, as their values become clearer and they verbalize them better, they get closer to a precise idea of what is essential to them.

On the scale for what she wanted in her next career, Sara gave High Income, Variety, Leadership, and Prestige each a seven. She gave Independence, Security, Challenge, and Creativity a six. Working in Your Main Field of Interest and Interpersonal Relationships scored fours, while she only gave Leisure and Helping Others threes. This totaled sixty-six points, almost twenty points over the maximum. She had to eliminate eighteen points to get to the required limit.

During Sara's second pass with the Values Scale, it was interesting to watch her process of elimination.

"I need a good income, but if I relocated to a less expensive area, I could probably get by on less than I have been, especially if the job had good potential down the road." So she changed her answer from a seven to a five.

Prestige was very important for her, and she was only willing to give up one point of that. She still felt strongly about Independence—she needed some control over her schedule to accommodate her children—but that it wasn't as much a factor if she relocated to someplace like Seattle, where her family lived, so she switched that to a four.

"After my divorce, I considered moving back there," she explained. "I decided against it then because I knew it would be difficult to reestablish my practice where no one knew me. It would

be different now. I don't have that problem. My folks are getting older, and my children have never been around an extended family. The cost of living there is a good deal lower than here. If I had to take a cut in income, it would certainly go a lot farther there."

Helping Others went from a three to a one.

"My whole life reflects my interest in helping others, from Cub Scouts, to after school programs, and reading for the blind. I've always done these things, and I expect I will continue. I don't feel I need this kind of fulfillment in a job."

She was non-negotiable around the issue of Security.

"Maybe I can get along on less money, but I have to have a dependable base salary, and I can grow from there."

Another important point was that she wanted some sense of identification with, of belonging to, an organization. She was not willing to negotiate on that.

Variety was important. The repetitiveness of her former job created the need for a new career. She didn't want to fall into that trap again. She went from a seven to a six and wasn't willing to go beyond that. She decided to bump Leadership from a seven to a five.

"When you start a new profession, you can't expect you're going to be in a position to assume a leadership role. I know I'll prove myself in time, and then I can expect to move into a leadership role."

She dropped the Interest field to a one because she believed she wanted to stay within the health care industry, so she didn't need to waste any points for that. She was becoming very, very stingy with her points.

She kept Leisure at a three because she still felt she needed to have time with her children. She changed Challenge by one point, reasoning that the challenge had been thrust upon her, and there was no need to actively go out and pursue it.

She reduced Interpersonal Relations by only one point, from a four to a three, because she felt she needed to look at a profession that was people-oriented. As a dental hygienist, she felt she had little opportunity to interact with people on a social level.

"People don't talk to you much while your hands are in their mouths."

73

Again she felt there were other avenues, other outlets for her Creativity, and she dropped that to a four.

The second total came within one point of the goal of forty-eight.

"Oh, boy. Now what do I do? I've already compromised as far as I can."

I held her to the task. It is important to take that last step. She finally struck through the number for Interpersonal Relations and moved that to a two.

"If I have to give up something, it will have to be the people orientation. I've done that before; I guess I can do it again."

This would not mean her job wouldn't be people-oriented, only that this wouldn't be uppermost in her criteria as she looked for careers.

As she worked and reworked this exercise, it became dramatically apparent that in the final analysis her highest values were Prestige, Security, and Variety. She could now take a look at potential careers with these in mind. The areas of compromise were Independence, High Income, Leadership, Challenge, and Interest Field because she felt all those would come as a result of the new profession.

Now that Sara was clear on her own values, she needed to use this information to analyze her opportunities. ＊

Smell the Coffee
Wishing Doesn't Make It So

The key here is to have a plan of action. First, look at your highest values. Use this information to analyze your opportunities based on how many of your priorities are part of the overall job. Now look at what you especially liked about your current position. Use the first values exercise to help you here. Then look at the downside, or the reasons for wanting to move on. Using these as benchmarks, take some time at the library, and see what you can learn about industries, careers, and specific positions that fit your values and your skills and experience (either that which you have, or that you are willing to get). Once you've identified interesting areas to explore, go back to your priorities. Do these incorporate your highest values? Now is the time to take off the rose-colored

74

glasses and determine what, if any, compromises will have to be made.

I sent Sara to the library with her benchmarks and assigned her many of the tasks you'll find in Chapter 6. When she returned, she had a wealth of information.

"I started with health care. It's a pretty big field. I looked at the dental side first. There are some surprising possibilities there, such as selling dental supplies. There are also dental hygienist schools, and that opened up another whole avenue. A couple I found interesting were recruiting and public relations."

She also looked outside the dental field, particularly in the sales field. Pharmaceutical and hospital supplies didn't seem so far from dentistry.

Now it was time to go back to her priorities. At the top of the list were Security, Prestige, and Variety. She also wanted a position with growth potential and the challenge of something new and different, but in a relatively safe environment. She enjoyed interpersonal relations with people and wanted to establish those.

"I don't want to be stuck behind a desk, staring into a computer all day," she said.

Sales was far and away her first choice.

"I've always been self-motivated. My income's always been based on my own motivation. It wouldn't be any different in sales."

She outlined a career path as she saw it.

"My first step would be as a front-line salesperson. From there, I could move to sales director and finally to regional sales manager. Sales has the greatest potential for regaining my income."

I admired her self-confidence, but felt she needed to face the reality that a "commission only" position would compromise one of her highest values, Security.

"You're right, that's more risk than I'm willing to take," she admitted. She flung herself back in her chair and looked up at the ceiling for a while.

"Not all sales positions are commission only," she concluded. "I would need to make that clear. I need the security of a regular paycheck, especially in a new field. It needn't be what

I've been making, especially if I move to Seattle, but I'd have to count on it."

Sara left that day with a plan in her head. Her first choice was to look for a sales position with a dental supply house. If nothing came from that, she would look for a position with a dental hygienist school, either in recruitment or public relations. If the dental field failed to produce for her, she would look into appropriate positions within the hospital supply and pharmaceutical fields.

*All the way through our work together, one particular element stood out. Sara had a strong sense of her Professional Self. She saw herself as a highly skilled individual; she had a very positive sense of self, and she felt quite confident that now that she had a game plan in hand, she could support herself and her children. She left looking forward to the challenge. ***

The Company and the World It Operates In
Corporate Values

Another set of work values you should keep in mind might be labeled "Corporate Values." Sometimes, this is reflected in the hierarchy of the company. Every job, especially at the management level, is shaped by the personal values, goals, and management style of the principal. Sometime during your working life, you will probably be faced with a work situation that requires you to evaluate the organization and the employer, based on how well they mesh with your own values.

I interviewed once for a position with a highly visible elected official. After a few minutes of chit chat, he asked how I had prepared for my interview.

"I checked you out," I said and told him how I had identified, contacted, and interviewed people in the community who knew him.

He was surprised.

"If you and I are going to work closely in as visible a position as this," I told him, "I need to feel comfortable with what you stand for, what is important to you. I need to understand whether there are any conflicts regarding our individual stands on issues I know will be raised if I work here."

He leaned forward in his chair, looked at me over the tops of his half-glasses, and asked, "Well, what did they say about me?"

"I'm here, aren't I?" I replied, and I got the job.

Sometimes, corporate culture reflects more the corporate atmosphere you'll work in, but it is no less important. Jenny's experience illustrates this.

*After she received her BA degree, and at her father's urging, she applied for a job at a bank. Her first assignment was as a teller. At this particular branch, the other tellers had little college experience. Dress tended toward short skirts and dramatic makeup. The cracking of chewing gum set her teeth on edge. Inept and unhappy behind the counter, she asked the manager to move her to accounting. This turned out to be no better. Jenny felt no closer to her co-workers, who delighted in showing off pictures of their grandchildren. Finally, the manager put her into a training program for loan officers. Here, she found the social companionship and age cohort she needed to feel comfortable with the job. *

Most organizations have a Code of Ethics or a Mission Statement that addresses the idea of corporate values and that are readily available on the company's website. Amway and Mary Kay, for instance, besides being highly successful business concepts, incorporate specific value systems they expect to be honored. Patagonia Industries donates a percentage of its annual profits to organizations that strive to preserve the environment. Ben and Jerry's Ice Cream has decided their CEO will earn only eight times what its lowest-paid worker makes. All of these are reflections of "corporate values." It is important, if you have strong feelings about certain issues, to research your potential employer with those feelings in mind. If they are in conflict, you must make some definite decisions regarding how much of your individual values and attitudes you are wiling to compromise to fit comfortably into the organization.

Business organizations struggle with issues of social responsibility and corporate values all the time. There are no easy answers on how to solve major social ills facing the world today. Many organizations do their best to prevent potential problems, but accidents do happen, and attempts to resolve the problems are fraught with conflict. Others believe this is beyond the purview of business and ignore these issues altogether. In any case, you should never work for a company or a person where your basic values are in conflict. It is not fair to either of you.

All of life is a series of choices. Having a strong sense of your own values, you can use these to make those choices that will give you the greatest satisfaction, not only personally, but as a high "emotional salary."

*Three months after I last met with Sara, I received a letter telling me she had settled into a house not far from her parents' home in Seattle and had accepted a position with a company that marketed prepaid dental plans. Last year's Christmas card included a note saying her year-end bonus put her just over the $85,000 mark, and she had made an offer on a house. *

Values Prioritization Exercise

Weigh each work value below on its importance to you, and circle the number that most closely reflects your feeling (higher number = more important).

HIGH INCOME. Some minimum income (enough for survival) is essential for everyone. But beyond that, how important to you are the extras? People have different ideas about how much income is "high." Therefore, *high income* is not defined here as a specific amount. It means more than enough to live on. It means money to use as you wish after you have paid your basic living expenses. You can buy luxuries and travel first class.

0   1   2   3   4   5   6   7   8

PRESTIGE. If people respect you, look up to you, listen to your opinions, or seek your help in community affairs, you are a person with *prestige*. Of course, *prestige* can be gained in several ways. But in present-day America, occupation is usually the key to *prestige*. Rightly or wrongly, we respect some occupations more than others.

0   1   2   3   4   5   6   7   8

INDEPENDENCE. Some occupations give you more freedom than others to make your own decisions, to work without supervision or direction from others. At one extreme might be talented freelance artists or writers who may work without supervision. At the other extreme might be military service or some big business organizations with chains or command which severely limit the decisions that each person can make.

0   1   2   3   4   5   6   7   8

HELPING OTHERS. Most people are willing to help others and do it every day outside of their work. They put themselves out to do favors, make gifts, donate to charities, and so on. *This does not count here.* The question here is: Do you want *Helping Others* to be a main part of your occupation? To what extent do you want to devote your life work directly to helping people improve their health, education, or welfare?

0   1   2   3   4   5   6   7   8

SECURITY. In the most secure occupations, you will be free from fear of losing your job and income. You will have tenure—that is, you cannot be fired very easily. Employment will tend to remain high despite recessions, and there will be no seasonal ups and downs. Your income will usually remain stable and predictable; it will not vanish with hard times. Your occupation is not likely to be wiped out by automation or other technological changes.

0   1   2   3   4   5   6   7   8

VARIETY. Occupations with the greatest *variety* offer many different kinds of activities and problems, frequent changes in location, new people to meet. *Variety* is the opposite of routine, predictability, or repetition. If you value *variety* high, you probably like novelty and surprise, and enjoy facing new problems, events, places, and people.

0   1   2   3   4   5   6   7   8

LEADERSHIP. Do you want to guide others, tell them what to do, be responsible for their performance? People who weigh *leadership* high usually want power to control events. They want to influence people to work together efficiently. If they are mature, they know that responsibility goes with *leadership*. They are willing to accept the blame when things go wrong, even though they were not at fault.

0   1   2   3   4   5   6   7   8

WORK IN YOUR MAIN FIELD OF INTEREST. Some people have only one main field of interest (science, engineering, business, helping others, writing, art, or music); others are interested in two or more fields. Some insist that their occupation must be in one of their major fields of interest. Others are willing to work in a field that is less interesting; they feel they can satisfy their main interest in their spare time.

0   1   2   3   4   5   6   7   8

LEISURE. How important is the amount of time your occupation will allow you to spend away from work? Leisure may include short hours, long vacations, or the chance to choose your own time off. To give a high weight to leisure is like saying, "The satisfactions I get off the job are so important to me that work must not interfere with them."

0   1   2   3   4   5   6   7   8

CHALLENGE. Some people feel more satisfied when they expend great effort in solving problems at work. The presence of a problem demands their attention. Are you bored with easy work and stimulated with more difficult tasks? Would you prefer to work on assignments requiring real learning and effort?

0   1   2   3   4   5   6   7   8

INTERPERSONAL RELATIONS. Some occupations provide the opportunity to deal with people. Some people like to be a part of a team and to participate with others. Would working alone be undesirable to you? Do you enjoy the chance to meet people?

0   1   2   3   4   5   6   7   8

CREATIVITY. In some occupations, you are encouraged to try out original solutions rather than rely on conventional tactics and established procedures. Are you proud of your ability to offer ideas in many situations? Do you have creative talents that you want to develop and use?

0   1   2   3   4   5   6   7   8

Scoring

For each section (1–12) enter your score under the column labeled "Initial Score." After the numbers have been entered, total the column. If the total exceeds a score of forty-eight, go back to each value and adjust or eliminate original scores under the column labeled "Adjusted Score." In a sense, you are ranking your values. This "Adjusted Score" should reflect those values about which you feel the strongest.

Values	Initial Score	Adjusted Score
(1) High Income	_____	_____
(2) Prestige	_____	_____
(3) Independence	_____	_____
(4) Helping Others	_____	_____
(5) Security	_____	_____
(6) Variety	_____	_____
(7) Leadership	_____	_____
(8) Interest Field	_____	_____
(9) Leisure	_____	_____
(10) Challenge	_____	_____
(11) Interpersonal Relations	_____	_____
(12) Creativity	_____	_____
Total Weight	_____	_____

1. What are your three highest values?

2. In what areas did you have to compromise?

*

"No person who is enthusiastic about his work has anything to fear from life." — Samuel Goldwyn

*

"Work is not primarily a thing one does to live, but the thing one lives to do. It is, or should be, the full expression of the worker's faculties, the thing in which he finds spiritual, mental and bodily satisfaction, and the medium in which he offers himself to God."
— Dorothy L. Sayers

*

"The secret of life is to have a task, something you bring everything to, every minutes of the day for your whole life. And the most important thing is— it must be something you cannot possibly do."
— Henry Moore

*

5   Identifying Your Personality Style
Using It to Create Career Satisfaction

Throughout your life, you'll have to deal with a number of different kinds of bosses, as well as peers and subordinates. An understanding of personality styles can help you improve your communications skills.

Maybe a job change is not warranted. Sometimes just knowing more about yourself and your co-workers will turn an impossible situation into a workable and rewarding one.

People with similar personality styles have a tendency to get along well and can accomplish a great deal. But there can be too much of a good thing. Like-minded people tend to miss out on a variety of perspectives that lend flavor, dimension, and balance to the workplace. The adage that "opposites attract" is a good rule of thumb in order to ensure maximum productivity. This is true only if we appreciate the unique contributions each person brings to the workplace and realize that in an effective working unit each special talent contributes to the attitude, climate, and productivity of the whole.

* Natalie Weiss-Gordon was full of rage when she first came to see me.

"Can you believe this?" She slammed a performance review down in front of me. "Never in my life have I been given a negative review. And he's pretty clear all right. He wants me out!"

What I observed before me was an attractive thirty-two-year-old woman, wholesome looking, well put together in a conservative mode. Underneath this bravado, she clearly felt embarrassed because of the situation that prompted her to come and see me.

As I reviewed the printed format with its handwritten notes sprawled within each section, Natalie calmed herself down.

"It's more than just a poor review," she admitted in a quiet voice. "I care deeply about this job, and I believe I have done a good job. No one indicated any different. I am truly shocked."

She offered some background.

After graduating from the University of Illinois in Public Administration and working as an administrative analyst for the Department of Health and Human Services in Chicago for five years, she accompanied her husband to California, where he took advantage of the then booming entertainment industry.

She immediately began looking at jobs with government agencies since that's what she knew, that's what she liked, and that's what she was comfortable with. Her past evaluations stood her in good stead, and within three months, she landed an excellent position within the criminal justice system in San Diego helping to administer a federal grant designated to teach parenting skills to women inmates who had a history of abusing their children.

"The grant is a result of the research done in the Minneapolis Domestic Violence Research Study," she told me, warming to her subject. "That study showed that battered women have a tendency to batter their children, and those children have a tendency to marry into battering relationships. It creates a cyclical effect on families. The way we see it, children coming from dysfunctional families don't receive good parenting. This grant could have long-term ramifications by intercepting battering women while they are in jail and helping them develop appropriate parenting skills. If they feel good about one aspect of their lives, they can build on that and potentially rehabilitate themselves in other ways. This could benefit their children and their children's children. It is an important program, and I want to stay involved."

"How did you get to this point?" I asked, holding up the evaluation sheet.

"There are two phases to the grant," she began. "The first is a two-year start-up period for developing the program and enlisting support from various law enforcement agencies. The second part is a three-year grant working with the actual inmates. At the end of this first phase, if the program doesn't meet both the programmatic and the enrollment requirements, the rest of the money will go to two other pilot programs, one in Philadelphia, the other in Maine, and that will be the end of it as far as this office is concerned."

When Natalie was offered the position, it was on a six-month probationary basis. This did not concern her, as she was confident in her ability.

She went to work for Ben Coburn, just three years out of a Master's program in Public Administration with emphasis in criminal justice and rehabilitation. The current grant was a continuation of the research for his Master's thesis. Ben's major responsibility in this phase consisted chiefly of meeting with different law enforcement agencies, determining the needs of the female inmates through interviews, and gaining the support of the agencies through convincing them of the program's value.

"I've just finished my probationary period," Natalie explained. "I've been pleased with the progress of the project and pleased with my part in it. I was actually looking forward to my first performance review!" Her anger rose again.

"Ben says I lack self-confidence, I'm not particularly verbal, and I need a great deal of supervision. He says I have potential to do the job, but he's not comfortable recommending me for a permanent position. He says he needs someone who is already capable, not someone with 'potential.'" She threw up her hands. "I cannot understand why, if Ben didn't like what I was doing, he never said anything to me. This is a real slap in the face."

"What did you do?"

"I refused to sign it. I went to the personnel office and asked to file a grievance charging poor supervision standards."

As part of the grievance process Natalie was required to discuss the evaluation with a career counselor, and that is what brought her here.

After extensive discussion of her reaction to the evaluation, I asked my bottom line question:

"What is it you want to happen as a result of this grievance?"

She was quite explicit. She wanted a new evaluation written with a clear understanding of what her strengths were and what benefits had accrued to the organization as a result of her being there, and she wanted some mediation and agreement between her and Ben as to her value and accomplishments. She chiefly felt that

87

without her organizational skills, Ben's creativity would be lost.

The next step was to get Ben's side of the story. When he entered my office, I was impressed, just in terms of the difference in appearance and presence between the two. He was a contemporary Californian, twenty-seven years old, blond, and tan. I could see why he did so well in his public appearances. Once he got on stage, it was obvious that he knew his stuff and presented it very well. I could see where his personable, boyish, "one of the guys" charm would be welcomed by the law enforcement officials. His entire approach communicated his message: "We have a way to help you stop the revolving door of mothers, children, and grandchildren going through your system. Together, let's make it happen."

I asked Ben to describe Natalie.

"She's a bean counter. She wants to make sure all our little ducks are in a row. She wants to make sure all the i's are dotted and t's are crossed all the time," he explained. "I see no point in doing any more of that than absolutely necessary. In most cases, I believe the process takes care of itself."

It became obvious that one of the problems was a clash of personality styles, a clash between the way each interacted with the world around them, how they perceived their work, and how they perceived others. *

There is a natural human tendency to try to understand and relate to others as if their inner world were like our own. Unfortunately, this is not often the case. It's important to be able to understand the natural differences in the way human beings think and act. To maximize your effectiveness, you must first understand your own personality style and what that means in terms of strengths and weaknesses. An excellent tool for determining this is the Myers–Briggs Type Indicator (MBTI). This is the world's most popular measure of personality dispositions. Well over 2 million people have used it.

The Myers–Brigs Type Indicator traces its roots back to the theories of Swiss-born psychiatrist C. G. Jung, who suggested that human behavior is not random but predictable, therefore classifiable. Jung went on to theorize that differences in behavior that seem so obvious to the naked eye are a result of preferences related to the basic functions that our personalities perform throughout life. These tendencies have to do with how we approach life, work, and problem solving. These preferences emerge early in life and form the basis of our personalities, and they become the core of our attractions to and aversions from people, tasks, and events throughout our lives.

Ask any parent to describe his or her children as infants. Parents are able to clearly distinguish and describe the different personality styles of each child from the day they bring it home from the hospital. They can easily describe which one of their children could sleep soundly in the midst of a thunder storm and which would wake at the slightest sound in the house, which sibling was engaging and willing to be held by other people and which one stuck closer to mom when new people were encountered. These differences are the beginning behaviors that demonstrate how our personalities affect how we navigate through our lives.

After Jung's scholarly work appeared in English in 1923, Katherine Briggs, in collaboration with her daughter, Isabel Briggs-Myers spent the better part of the next decade trying to perfect a way to easily use Jung's theory in counseling situations—thus the birth of the Myers–Briggs Type Indicator, the grandmother of a myriad group of personality analysis systems. It is frequently used in business and professional settings where people work in groups and need to deal constructively with differences.

For the career changer, these indicators help you understand that much of your attraction toward the tasks and responsibilities is the result of preferences developed early in life. They help you identify and understand these preferences, and you can use that information to identify the kinds of enterprises, positions, and corporate atmospheres that will provide your Professional Self with the most suitable climate for an enjoyable and meaningful work experience. I use this exercise twice in my career-counseling process, once during the preliminary stages of personal exploration, and then again as we prepare for the interview. It gives my clients the "booster shot" of confidence through self-awareness that ultimately leads to good interviews and from that to good job offers.

The indicators identify sixteen possible personality types, depending on how you measure along four specific dimensions:

1. Extrovert/Introvert looks at where we get our energy.
2. Sensing/Intuitive looks at how we get information from the world.
3. Thinking/Feeling looks at how we make decisions.
4. Judging/Perceiving looks at how we deal with the world.

The inventory helps you understand how you are likely to do your job, with what work environment you are most comfortable, how you like to take in information and make decisions, and where you focus your attention. It helps you understand the kind of temperament you have, what combination of psychological and professional strengths you offer. For the most complete interpretation, take this inventory under the guidance and interpretation of a trained career counselor. For a quick look at yourself and others around you, try the Personality Style Inventory at the end of this chapter.

In each pair of traits, Natalie possessed the attributes of one, Ben of the other, a totally mismatched pair. Natalie turned out to be an ISTJ, which means she was Introverted, Sensing, Thinking, and Judging. She was a classic Stabilizer in an organization, one of the people who like to organize things and preserve tradition, emphasizing efficiency and attention to detail and a systematized approach to everything. She was an analytical manager of facts and details, dependable, decisive, painstaking, stable, and conservative.

Ben, on the other hand, was an ENFP, an Extroverted, Intuitive, Feeling, Perceiving person. He exemplified the Catalyst, someone who is creative, imaginative, and individualistic in his approach to others. He was a warmly enthusiastic planner of change, individualistic; he pursued inspiration with impulsive energy and endeavored to understand and inspire others.

"Ben is always out in front making speeches, shaking hands, getting the law enforcement agencies to sign on to this program, yet nothing ever gets done back at the office because he is too busy doing those things," Natalie said. "We're going to be audited in another eight months. My concern is that if we don't get our facts and figures in order, we are going to lose funding for the rest of the grant. As Assistant Director, I feel I have the responsibility for making sure this is happening. Ben says I'm too detail-oriented and not terribly creative, that I jump the gun in making decisions." She paused, then continued, "But somebody has to make the decisions."

Ben's view was predictably different. When I asked Ben to give me his honest opinion of Natalie, he sat back and thought about it for a while. I could tell he was struggling with a lot of things. When he finally began, he spoke slowly, thoughtfully.

"You know I was part of the interview team that hired Natalie. We interviewed quite a few people. She wasn't my first choice, but I agreed to hire her because I thought she was good. Her evaluations from previous employers were stellar. She had great experience with the governmental process, and although I thought she was a little too conservative and quiet, I believed she was going to be very good for the project, and that's what disappoints me so much. We just don't seem to be on the same wavelength. I know she wants this program to work. I want this program to work. But I just don't know how we can make it work together."

*Both Natalie and Ben were competent individuals, and yet their work was becoming dysfunctional because they did not understand where the other was coming from. In every major aspect of how they looked at life, their approaches were diametrically opposed. ***

Extroverts tend to talk first and think later. They like being around groups of people both at work and socially, and they crave approval. An estimated 75 percent of all adults are Extroverts. Because they so greatly outnumber Introverts, they often fail to realize that such a thing as introversion even exists.

And Introverts do act differently from Extroverts. They often develop a high level of concentration and can block out distractions. They also like people, but more on a one-to-one basis. They don't like having their privacy invaded. Although often considered "good listeners," they can also be perceived as aloof, shy, and sometimes even arrogant.

*   * In the beginning, Ben had taken Natalie with him as a partner to make presentations and help gather information. Although Natalie's presentations were adequate, it was quickly apparent to Ben that it was not easy or natural for her to speak in front of a group. He was disappointed that she was unable to reach the audiences as well as he did. As time went on, he found himself leaving her behind more and more frequently, and he interpreted this as failure on her part. On the other hand, when he left her at the office, it only caused more trouble.*

"When she's there, she wants to run everything," he complained. "She is the Assistant Director. She's constantly reworking budgets and doing things I am responsible for."

*Ben resented Natalie's deciding without consulting him first. Natalie was appalled at Ben's not making decisions at all. Ben, on the other hand, had expected his assistant to help with the presentations. As an Extrovert, he didn't see this as any problem. He derived his energy from being around a lot of people, and he assumed everyone else did, too. He was a natural at public speaking and wanted her to be as excited about making presentations as he was. He just couldn't understand or relate to her discomfort. **

In determining how we choose to gather data or information from the world, the differences between the Sensing and Intuitive aspects were equally as wide. Sensors more often choose occupations where they can achieve practical results with tangible things. Intuitives generally prefer to give general answers to questions and are annoyed when people push them for detail. Their concentration tends to be scattered, and their friends often accuse them of being absentminded. On the other hand, Sensors have been accused of nit-picking.

I told Ben that one of Natalie's primary concerns was there had not been enough attention to detail regarding the audit. Ben very matter-of-factly said he had set aside the last month of the first phase to work on the audit and that he didn't want to look at much of it until then.

Intuitives are more frequently found among psychotherapists, strategic planners, philosophy professors, and lawyers—those occupations where there are no right or wrong answers. If you are a Sensor and your supervisor is more on the Intuitive side, the supervisor may misinterpret your asking a lot of detail questions before beginning an assignment as lack of confidence or inability to perform the job functions. All the while, you may see the supervisor's lack of clear direction as poor or weak leadership. It may be misinterpreted on your part as unprofessional management style. This is an easy trap to fall into if you are an Intuitive, as it is estimated that 70 percent of the U.S. population are Sensors.

The same kinds of conflicts are apt to present themselves in how Thinkers and Feelers typically make decisions in their lives. Thinkers are likely to assume that logic applies to everyone and that those who don't operate this way are simply using logic poorly. They tend to behave independently within their own internal mechanisms to come up with enough pros and cons to be comfortable making decisions. They've been accused of being cold and uncaring.

Feelers don't like conflict and tend to be accommodating. They make decisions using a very personalized, subjective, values-driven process. They tend to be ruled by compassion rather than logic. Thinkers often consider them wishy-washy. If you are the only Feeler in a group of Thinkers, you will undoubtedly feel persecuted and put upon at work. You will not understand their matter-of-fact way of doing business and be somewhat alarmed by what you observe as their callous way of making decisions.

Men have traditionally been thought of as Thinkers and women as Feelers. However, this is not as lopsided as once presumed. Recent surveys have shown that about 40 percent of men are feelers, and about 40 percent of women are Thinkers.

The last two sets of preferences take a look at how people tend to orient their lives.

*Ben was a Perceiver. It was very difficult for him to make decisions because he was an information gatherer. Every time he reached a point where he had to make a critical judgment, as far as Natalie saw it, he went out in the field to get more information. This caused one of the major bones of contention between the two. *

As you can see, this aspect of their personalities reflected the way they preferred to interact with the world and the way they preferred to receive stimulation and energy.

*Natalie was a Judger. She was decisive, firm, and sure. She set goals and stuck to them. Decisions came easily to her, but, according to Ben, she made decisions without enough information. Like most Judgers, Natalie wanted to close the books and get on to the next project. When a project does not yet have closure, Judgers often leave it behind and go on to new tasks and don't look back. *

Judgers have a tendency to be regimented, and they don't like surprises. They are sometimes accused of being angry when they're only stating an opinion.

Perceivers often believe they do not make good decisions because of a sense of foreboding that overcomes them once they reach a point of committing themselves to a decision. They begin to think about the possibilities they have eliminated, the options that are no longer available, and they spend a lot of time contemplating the "what ifs." Their forte is information and opinion gathering, but when it comes down to deciding, they become very uncomfortable and tend to shy away, opting to gather more information.

Decision making will never be easy for Perceivers. It helps, however, if they can understand that their discomfort stems from the process of decision making, not necessarily from making poor decisions. This understanding will enable them to develop coping strategies that can make the process less stressful and increase their effectiveness as decision makers. It is important to get them to understand that they can and will make good judgments but at the same time acknowledge that there will always be a certain amount of discomfort when they do.

These last two characteristics are the most evenly divided. In the general population, 55 percent of people have a judging preference, whereas 45 percent are Perceivers.

Some combinations of these eight characteristics are found more frequently among certain occupations. For instance, in a recent study of lawyers, more than half are represented by just four of the possible sixteen types, and three of those four included the Thinker–Judger combination. The Sensor–Feeler combination is often found among psychologists. Some common characteristics of the various personality styles will be found at the end of the chapter.

Meanwhile, Natalie and Ben continued to work together at the office under an agreement that they not discuss their differences. I wanted them to think about the differences and their strengths and weaknesses independently, without input from the other or from their co-workers. I suggested that Ben continue his speaking engagements and, at least for now, he allow Natalie to review the budgets in preparation for the audit, giving her some relief from her anxiety over not being prepared.

After reviewing the results of the MBTI, I recommended that we meet with a representative of the personnel department. Prior to the meeting I sat down with Ben and Natalie independently and thoroughly discussed their individual personality styles, their competencies and limitations, and what each style brought to the organization.

The ultimate goal of their working together was to preserve, modify, and improve the working relationship so as to ensure the adequate functioning of the grant. It was very similar to couples counseling in that individuals within the couple need to understand that if the relationships is to continue, there needs to be compromise and understanding on both parts. Neither is wrong; neither is right. They need to understand what their differences are, come to some kind of mutual accord in terms of how each is going to accept and respect those differences and work with them. They need to develop a working relationship that plays on the strengths of each and mitigates the weaknesses.

Ben and Natalie represent an extreme but not uncommon case. They also had the benefit of a personnel department that referred them to a trained career counselor. As you look at your own situation, you may find yourself on your own. *

Knowledge Is Power
Working Effectively with Diversity

To understand the dynamics in your own work situation, see how well the results of the exercise at the end of the chapter fit the way you approach life, work, and problem solving.

Next, identify the characteristics of the person or persons at work who are contributing to your discomfort. See if these characteristics fit a personality style in conflict with yours. Ask yourself,

1. "How do I feel about people who operate with this style?"
2. "How do I usually relate with these people?"
3. "What can I do to deal more effectively with this style?"

Start by identifying and appreciating the strengths of this style. Then look at the weaknesses and see what can be done to minimize your conflict. Do your best to work out your differences. It will help you determine whether it is feasible to remain in your present situation. You can decide if you want to accommodate the other person. You can ask to be accommodated. You might want to seek the aid of a career counselor to help you clarify the issues you are dealing with and work out a solution.

The above is a good exercise to practice with the variety of personality styles you come in contact with on a daily basis. This can have far-reaching effects. Throughout your life, you'll have to deal with a number of different kinds of bosses, as well as peers and subordinates. An understanding of personality styles can help you improve your communications skills, especially when you or someone else has one of the less frequent characteristics. For instance, you can adapt your own style of communication to be more like that of the individual you're trying to influence. It can also help you in dealing with clients, or marketing your services to a prospective client. You'll be able to step back, understand how the person's type preferences appear to differ from your own, and adjust your communication in a way he or she can most easily accept. Your overall success will increase in proportion to how well you work with each of these situations. You'll make yourself, as well as everyone else, look good.

I met with Ben and Natalie again independently before the meeting, and with their consent, discussed the other's results and how that affected their relationship and their ability to work with each other. They began to understand that there were no pathological or psychological malfunctions on the part of either.

Prior to the meeting, I also asked them to recommend to me how they would restructure their work responsibilities to highlight their own strengths and minimize their weaknesses. I asked them to come up with four recommendations and submit them to me in writing. I reviewed them, incorporated my own recommendations, and then presented the package to them and the personnel officer all at once. By this time, Natalie and Ben had an opportunity to understand their differences and were beginning to feel less hostile toward each other.

"First, let me suggest the position of Assistant Director be rewritten and that the Assistant Director assume primary responsibility for record keeping and report writing for the purpose of grant requirements and auditing. As Director, Ben, you will still be able to review and approve the final draft."

This left Ben's power intact, but made the process easier for them both and gave Natalie something solid to bite into.

"I also feel the Assistant Director should be able to develop the necessary systems and support to provide the appropriate documentation for the grant reporting."

Having this in writing gave Natalie the permission she needed to develop these without having to bug Ben with detail questions. In effect, it allowed the process to take care of itself via Natalie.

"I think everyone will be more comfortable if you remove Natalie's responsibility for public presentations from the job description."

I suggested that once a week they meet, over a two-hour lunch, to discuss both long- and short-term assignments. This provided structure for Ben in a manner he could accept because of the informality of lunch. Natalie would give Ben a list of things that needed to be accomplished by the end of the month. She presented goals rather than structure. However he chose to accomplish those goals was then his decision.

These meetings gave Natalie the structure she needed. She knew with certainty that on Friday afternoons, for two hours she had Ben's undivided attention. I worked with Natalie and Ben twice more and they began to develop a remarkable sense of respect for what each of them brought to the project. And while they never saw eye to eye on everything, Ben became much more confident in Natalie's ability to handle matters; Natalie became much less critical of Ben's style and much more appreciative of his flamboyance and creativity. They truly became working partners as each strove to become supportive of the other, ensuring that both shone like the stars they were.

*As a result, Ben rewrote the evaluation, and Natalie dropped her complaint about his management style. The project flourished under this new working relationship. ***

If you decide a career change is necessary, this knowledge of personality styles will be an invaluable guide in choosing your next employer. For instance, by paying attention to personality styles, you will have an early warning system as to how your new boss is likely to operate. You can then tailor your interview responses in the most effective terms, giving the most appropriate information for that style. On the other hand, you may be able to decide quickly, based on the style you see, that this would not be a workable situation and move on.

Another way I have found information on personality styles very helpful is in finding co-workers who fill in the gaps of your own personality style. If you have weaknesses in a certain area, find that co-worker who has the opposite dimension and trade strengths, as it were. For most of my professional life, I have had as one of my co-workers a man who was as much of a Sensor as I am Intuitive. I am very creative, deal with possibilities, and bore quickly with detail. I have lots of good ideas, often too many to implement, but that has never stopped me from having them. My co-worker was a planner. I would run into his office with my latest idea for a workshop or program for students, and invariably get peppered with questions about content, marketing, handouts, detail, detail, detail. Often, I accused him of trying to take the wind out of my sails until I realized one day that if I was ever really going to get these programs off the ground I would need to sit down and plan them, however odious I thought that particular activity was. Over the years, Alex and I planned and executed many successful programs for students, and he was respected on our staff as being the most Sensing of the whole bunch. Often, our discussions involving programming would include actively seeking Alex's input on the feasibility of our programs. My dear friend and co-worker died in 2006 at the tender age of 56 of complications from diabetes; so for the past year I have been without my Sensor at work. The number of times I have thought about stepping into his office to run an idea past him has begun to subside, and I am starting to look at the other Sensors in the office to fill in my sensing needs. My friend and co-worker will always be for me the quintessential Sensor. So Alex, this one's for you!

Personal Style Inventory

Visit the website below in order to find the Personal Style Inventory based on D.W. Champagne and R. C. Hogan:

www.utmem.edu/fammed/personalstyleinventory.doc

Use the space on the next few pages to write in your answers to the questions found on the website.

I prefer:

1a. _____
1b. _____

2a. _____
2b. _____

3a. _____
3b. _____

4a. _____
4b. _____

5a. _____
5b. _____

6a. _____

6b. _____

7a. _____

7b. _____

8a. _____

8b. _____

9a. _____

9b. _____

10a. _____

10b. _____

11a. _____

11b. _____

12a. _____

12b. _____

13a. _____

13b. _____

14a. _____

14b. _____

15a. _____

15b. _____

16a. _____

16b. _____

17a. _____

17b. _____

18a. _____

18b. _____

19a. _____

19b. _____

20a. _____

20b. _____

21a. _____

21b. _____

22a. _____

22b. _____

23a. _____

23b. _____

24a. _____

24b. _____

25a. _____

25b. _____

26a. _____

26b. _____

27a. _____

27b. _____

28a. _____

28b. _____

29a. _____

29b. _____

30a. _____

30b. _____

31a. _____

31b. _____

32a. _____

32b. _____

Personal Style Inventory Scoring Sheet

Instructions: Transfer your scores for each item of each pair to the appropriate blanks. Be careful to check the a and b letters to be sure you are recording the right blank spaces. Then total the scores for each dimension. The letter with the highest number in each dimension indicates your style for that area. You will end up with a four-letter code, one from each dimension that will identify your personal style.

DIMENSION		DIMENSION	
I	E	N	S
Item	Item	Item	Item
1b. _____	1a. _____	2a. _____	2b. _____
5a. _____	5b. _____	6b. _____	6a. _____
9a. _____	9b. _____	10a. _____	10b. _____
13a. _____	13b. _____	14a. _____	14b. _____
17a. _____	17b. _____	18a. _____	18b. _____
21b. _____	21a. _____	22a. _____	22b. _____
25b. _____	25a. _____	26b. _____	26a. _____
29b. _____	29a. _____	30a. _____	30b. _____

TOTAL

I _____   E _____   N _____   S _____

DIMENSION   DIMENSION

T	F	P	J
Item	Item	Item	Item
3a. _____	3b. _____	4a. _____	4b. _____
7a. _____	7b. _____	8a. _____	8b. _____
11a. _____	11b. _____	12a. _____	12b. _____
15a. _____	15b. _____	16a. _____	16b. _____
19b. _____	19a. _____	20b. _____	20a. _____
23b. _____	23a. _____	24b. _____	24a. _____
27a. _____	27b. _____	28a. _____	28b. _____
31b. _____	31a. _____	32b. _____	32a. _____

TOTAL

T _____   F _____   P _____   J _____

My Personal Style code is   _____ _____ _____ _____

Personality Styles in the Workplace

Introverts

Like quiet time for concentration.
Tend to be careful with details; dislike sweeping statements.
Have trouble remembering names and facts.
Tend not to mind working on one project for a long time without interruption.
Are interested in the idea behind their job.
Dislike telephone intrusions and interruptions.
Like to think a lot before they act, sometimes without acting.
Work contentedly alone.
Have some problems communicating.

Extroverts

Like variety and action.
Tend to be faster; dislike complicated procedures.
Are often good at greeting people.
Are often impatient with long, slow jobs.
Are interested in the results of their job, in getting it done, and in how other people do it.
Often do not mind the interruption of answering the telephone.
Often act quickly, sometimes without thinking.
Like to have people around.
Usually communicate freely.

Sensing Types

Dislike new problems unless there are standard ways to solve them.
Like an established way of doing things.
Enjoy using skills already learned more than learning new ones.
Work more steadily, with a realistic idea of how long it will take.
Usually reach a conclusion step by step.
Are patient with routine details.

Are impatient when details get complicated.
Are more often inspired, and rarely trust the inspiration when they are.
Seldom make errors of fact.
Tend to be good at precise work.

Intuitive Types

Like solving new problems.
Dislike doing the same thing repeatedly.
Enjoy learning a new skill more than using it.
Work in bursts of energy powered by enthusiasm, with slack periods in between.
Reach a conclusion quickly.
Are impatient with routine details.
Are patient with complicated situations.
Follow their inspirations, good or bad.
Frequently make errors of fact.
Dislike taking time for precision.

Thinking Types

Do not show emotion readily, and are often uncomfortable dealing with people's feelings.
May hurt people's feelings without knowing it.
Like analysis and putting things into logical order. Can get along without harmony.
Tend to decide impersonally, sometimes paying insufficient attention to people's wishes.
Need to be treated fairly.
Are able to reprimand people or fire them when necessary.
Are more analytically oriented—respond more easily to people's thoughts.
Tend to be firm-minded.

Feeling Types

Tend to be very aware of other people and their feelings.
Enjoy pleasing people, even in unimportant things.
Like harmony. Efficiency may be disturbed by office feuds.
Often let decisions be influenced by their own or other people's personal likes and wishes.

Need occasional praise.

Dislike telling people unpleasant things.

Are more people-oriented—respond more easily to people's values.

Tend to be sympathetic.

Judging Types

Work best when they can plan their work and follow the plan.

Like to get things settled and finished.

May decide things too quickly.

May dislike to interrupt the project they are on for a more urgent one.

May not notice new things that need to be done.

Want only the essentials needed to begin their work.

Tend to be satisfied once they reach a judgment on a thing, situation, or person.

Perceptive Types

Adapt well to changing situations.

Do not mind leaving things open for alterations.

May have trouble making decisions

May start too many projects and have difficulty in finishing them.

May postpone unpleasant jobs.

Want to know all about a new job.

Tend to be curious, and welcome new light on a thing, situation, or person.

For more information about the Myers–Briggs Type Indicator and how to use that information during career planning, you might want to look at the following books.

Kroeger and Thuesen. *Type Talk at Work: How the 16 Personality Types Determine Your Success on the Job.*

Dunning, Donna. *What's Your Type of Career? Unlock the Secrets of Your Personality to Find Your Perfect Career Path.*

Tieger and Barron-Tieger. *Do What You Are. Discover the Perfect Career for You Through the Secrets of Personality Type.*

1. **Learn to use resources already available in your community.**

2. **Frame your career search in the context of a world economy.**

3. **Learn specific techniques for exploring industries and positions.**

4. **Experience the powerful feeling of control and choice.**

Part II

Exploring and Researching the Job Market

6   Researching Your Options
Identifying and Targeting the Markets

"Many career changers, who wouldn't think of buying a car or a computer without doing exhaustive research, know almost nothing about the company they are pursuing."

Most people start their job search by looking for positions. They immediately begin searching the want ads for a job. They see little opportunity, and discouragement immediately sets in. They can't find anything in the want ads or the search engines because they don't know what they are looking for or they are looking for the same kind of job they are trying to get away from. Searching for positions should be fourth on your list as you begin to research the job market. Your first need is to gain perspective. You need to increase you knowledge base about the world of work so that you can make good decisions regarding the career moves you are going to make. You have got to become a better Career Consumer. What is happening in the global economy that is going to affect my job here in my hometown? How is this going to matter in terms of job security or the kinds of work I want to do? What is happening nationally? How will elections and who wins those elections affect the job market? For that matter, what is happening in my own community? What industries are ebbing or flowing? In the flourishing industries, which companies will be the leaders and which of those companies do I want to work for?

> ** Barbara Matteu bounded into my office, shook my hand, plopped herself into the chair, and immediately tucked one foot under the casual jeans she was wearing. The athletic six foot woman took up a lot of room in my tiny office. She was a friendly but imposing presence. She was one of those people that command a presence in a room. I was immediately curious about why she was here.*
>
> *"I'm twenty-nine years old, and I need some direction in my life," she began. "I've done a lot of things so far. I've supported myself since I left high school. I've traveled through most of the U.S. I've shod horses in Montana, cooked on a freighter on the Mississippi, and strung racquets at a country club*

in Atlanta. I went back to school and discovered I had two passions: biology and art. I graduated last spring with a double major."

"And now you need a job."

"Not just any job. I'm older now; I'll be thirty in the spring. I want to settle down. I want something stable: something for the long haul." She straightened her leg from under her and leaned forward. "I'm lean and mean and ready for somebody to reap the benefits of not only my education, but of my state of mind. And I don't know how to go about finding that." *

Many career changers, who wouldn't think of buying a car or a computer without doing exhaustive research, know almost nothing about the company they are pursuing, who runs it, what the prospects are for its immediate future, or for its industry as a whole. To be successful, it is imperative that you take a look at the overall job market and get an idea of where you fit in. It's about as much fun as looking for a car, but the rewards are just as tangible. **This research usually transcends all aspects of your career search and should begin the moment you decide you want to make a change.**

But what do you look for, and how do you know when you have found it? Once you have found it, how do you use it?

- By looking at global trends and national issues, you establish a context for your search.
- You'll use that knowledge to identify industries that will prosper in light of these trends.
- Then look for growing industries that mesh with your interests and are in the geographical preference area you have identified.
- From here, you'll explore the variety of positions available in those industries that integrate your interest areas and skill sets.
- Finally, you'll investigate specific employers who have job openings you will actively apply for.

You will now begin to integrate all of the information you have so diligently gathered during the Personal Assessment phase of the Professional Self Model. Researching the job market is a futile activity unless you are armed with information about what interests you. Information about yourself will help you discern which of the myriad of events might impact things you want to do. You are becoming a good Career Consumer by learning how to sift information you receive through regular daily interaction with the world at large. Your knowledge base about yourself as a working person has become clearer. You are able to focus more on the specifics of a particular profession because you know what skills you will be marketing in this particular job search. You know what your income needs are since you have looked at your values and made some clear statements about what you want and need in your next position. The hard part is sticking to the decisions that are driven by this new information and waiting for the right one to emerge from the numerous positions you will be applying for.

Start with some very general resources. Read the business section of your daily newspaper and all of weekly magazines like *Time* and *U.S. News & World Report.* These weekly news magazines are even broken down by sections called world news, national, business, arts and entertainment, and other industry-related titles. I always like to look at the personality profiles or features on people these magazines have. I have picked up some amazing information including names of CEOs, private philanthropies, corporations, information and contacts that could really add to a good job search. Look for information. Once you start reading these regularly, the sections will require only brief scanning for you to decide whether the information is pertinent to you. If you are more comfortable doing this on your computer, go right ahead and dig into their websites instead of reading their hard copies. For me, it is still more gratifying to stretch out on the couch in front of the fireplace and read *Newsweek* than it is to sit at the computer reading from a screen, but to each his own. Get acquainted with professional journals and business and industry guides. See what your library has to offer. Go to some of your favorite websites for information. Career-based websites are often treasure troves of articles on just about every aspect of the job search you will need to know. *Career Builder* and *Career Journal* are two websites I refer to frequently for work with students and to update my own knowledge base. Cruise these sites regularly, once or twice a week. Remember, you are trying to learn new behaviors as they relate to becoming more knowledgeable about the job market. The information will become easier to assimilate into your own bank of knowledge as you continue the practice.

Basically, you want to train your mind to recognize and accept information about careers and economic trends that is readily available as a part of your daily life. You need to train yourself to become a *career consumer*. Think of yourself as a detective as you search out these trends. You need to develop a "third eye," a career focus, if you will, with which to view the world. As you begin to filter information through this third eye, everything you read will be career-oriented; you'll see opportunities everywhere. But until it becomes part of your regular repertoire, the information is just going to bounce right off you as if it hit a Teflon shield. Aim for the Velcro effect, where the information sticks.

As you become more facile at conducting employer research and organizing your materials, it will become obvious the kind of information you will need and what is the quickest and easiest way to access that information. Look at this part of your job search as developing new skills that will improve your problem-solving and information-gathering techniques. Think of yourself as an investigator, hot on the trail of "The Hidden Job Market." Sure. You'll run into some red herrings and some leads will be dead ends, but the clues will begin to build on one another. And in the end, you'll unravel it all and come to a successful conclusion.

As you begin your research, you need to develop a system for keeping information straight. Notes, comments, and thoughts regarding the trends, industries, companies, and positions you will be learning about should be cataloged and organized in a way that will help you evaluate how they fit your current needs.

Keep a journal on the information you read, and give yourself a two-week deadline for your first intensive foray into career research. Deadlines are important when people are beginning the general part of a job search as they make them accountable and head off procrastination. At this point, the initial information might not seem relevant. As you develop a framework for it, you will find little hooks on which to hang each bit of information. As you progress, the information you derived from this preliminary investigation will become more important and valuable to you, and it will form the foundation for information yet to come.

What in the World Is Going On?
Global Issues

It should come as no surprise that we live in a global economy. Car parts are manufactured all over the world and gathered in one place for assembly. To assume that international events don't have an effect on local economies is folly. Regularly reading news magazines will give you significant information on the kids of global happenings that will affect you in the marketplace. For instance, as companies struggle to control domestic labor costs, more positions become available overseas. Through international trade agreements like GATT and NAFTA, our trading borders have exploded. The break-up of the communist bloc alone opened up 30 percent of the world to new economic opportunities. These countries in Eastern Europe are ripe with entrepreneurial opportunities for the truly adventurous. Working with international nonprofit groups or for nongovernmental organizations (NGOs) on issues of human interest all over the world now gives us more opportunities to ply our skills on the global level. Private philanthropies like the Bill and Melinda Gates Foundation are tackling health issues on a global scale. To do this, their organization is constantly in need of skilled, trained, and capable workers from many disciplines. Foreign and domestic companies have rewritten personal policies, and work visas are more broadly written to try and accommodate the world economy's need for workers. China is the fastest-growing economy in today's world. The need for people who speak multiple languages and understand different cultures and ways of doing business will continue to increase as we continue to define what work is in our lives. How do we make sense of all this information?

Remember I talked about the idea of Perspective? In doing job market research for an impending career change, it is important to take a fresh look at things. We get stuck looking at things in the same old way, and it is hard to see the forest for the trees. You need to refresh your thinking with information that will force you to think in different ways about your place in the world of work. One of the main goals of the Professional Self Model is to give people an opportunity to make good choices about their careers. I believe in order to do that you need to expand your horizons and imagine yourself differently. One of the best ways to enhance this process is to start imputing new information into your database, as it were. Change your perspective about work and who you are as a working person, and I believe the information you begin to incorporate through this job market research will start to stick and make sense. I have seen it work over and over again.

Make sure you have some people you are able to talk with during this career search. Being able to talk about all you are learning helps you incorporate it better. It gives you a chance to test out your new career vocabulary, and it will give you another person's perspective on the information you are sharing. Working with a career counselor is the optimum situation. It is important for you to acknowledge that there are times when it's best to call in the help of the professionals. You wouldn't try and fix your own teeth would you? I bet you wouldn't want to try and take out your own tonsils either? I bet most of you think it is absolutely appropriate to join a gym or hire a personal trainer to keep up good health. Why is it, then, that we are willing let something as important as what we do for a living be decided by the fates rather than have it be a conscious decision made after work with a career professional? If career counseling is not available, many community colleges over career courses through their regular curriculum and through their adult education classes. This process is a lot more stimulating and often moves more quickly when there is interaction with professionals and other career changers.

The goal here is to relate economic and global trends and issues to the information you have gathered about your Professional Self. It's important to look at this information at the very beginning of a job search as it helps you create an attitude that you have choices, and this gives you power.

I could see Barbara was not enthusiastic about all that reading.

"I'm not asking you to read everything from cover to cover," I assured her. "Sample everything and take only the information you feel is valuable or interesting. Read the books in your leisure time. Take them to the beach. Leave yourself time to assimilate and process what they have to offer."

Barbara arrived in my office two weeks later in a state of confusion.

"I am totally saturated with all the stuff I've soaked up. I feel like a sponge," she admitted as she again flung herself into the chair.

"Which book made the biggest impression on you?" I asked.

"Far and away it was Megatrends 2000. *Two of the major directions they talk about are the renaissance of the arts and the resurgence of the physical sciences such as biology. Here, all of a sudden, I find a national best seller confirming both my major fields!"*

*This was what I was hoping for—that out of these there would be one or two items that stood out as having information specifically useful to her. *

What's Good in the USA Is Good for Me
National Trends

Now take a look at what's going on here at home. National politics and their swings have a significant effect on economic sectors. Republican agendas tend to be more internationally based, defense aligned, more economically or business-oriented. Democratic agendas tend to focus on domestic, social, and education issues. Whoever is in the driver's seat will affect the kinds of economies that are going to matter on the job front. In any given year, budgets decided on in Washington, D.C., profoundly affect the kinds of jobs that are out there. If, for instance, you are looking for a research grant from the National Endowment of the Arts, you'd have a better chance at winning it under a Democratic Congress. If you were looking for a grant from the National

Security Council, you'll have better luck under a Republican regime. I want you to understand I am painting national politics with very broad strokes here but I hope you see that overall history will prove this out.

Current demographics are equally important. Take the Baby Boomers, for example. According to an Associated Press analysis of 2000 census data, Baby Boomers (those born between 1946 and 1964) now make up nearly one-third of the U.S. population. As they age, the marketplace is looking for what they will want. As a group, they have created another baby boom, although family size is generally smaller than a generation ago. They are in their prime earning years. They are also in their prime spending years, as they buy homes and prepare for college costs. New spending patterns indicate, for instance, that restaurants serving health-conscious food are becoming more popular, and even fast food chains have responded with leaner items on the menu. Health and safety issues are growing concerns. More emphasis is being placed on prevention and healthy aging, which creates opportunities for all kinds of new business to emerge to meet this trend in the population.

Whole new industries and governmental agencies have been started as a result of the bombing of the World Trade Centers and the War on Terror. Security agencies, electronic surveillance equipment, and the systems to support those services have created thousands of new positions worldwide. Humanitarian efforts in war-torn and drought-ridden areas continue to provide opportunities for people to work at meeting basic human needs. In laboratories around the world, scientists are working to improve food productivity and increase the amount of potable water available in the world.

In the next ten years, the forty-five-to-fifty-four age group will increase 44 percent, according to the Census Bureau. These will be predominately white, driving the demand for medical and leisure services, restaurants, and financial and retirement planning. The growth in the younger generation will be increasingly nonwhite, with Hispanics growing at the fastest rate. What will be their needs?

In recessions, when massive layoffs become the news of the day, some industries prosper, out-placement counseling for instance. Discount retail stores, low-cost leisure activities such as bowling and pool, DVD and game rentals, and fast food eateries tend to do well. One entrepreneurial hair salon profited from the most recent recession by positioning itself as a moderate-priced full-service salon, and attracted the newly cost conscious who still wanted maximum service.

To help her understand the possibilities, I asked Barbara to look for job and career fairs that focused on professional positions. These fairs are often listed in your local paper in the classified section under "employment," or you might find them advertised at career centers, your local state employment center, the Small Business Administration, or the chamber of commerce.

Barbara came racing back to my office after seeing a hundred or so employers at one job fair in the Los AngelesConvention Center. She was both excited and frustrated.

"I think I could work for at least half of them and be happy. How can I narrow down what I am looking for in an organization, and how can I become more comfortable with my choices? I don't want to start jumping around again. I want to settle down, join a company where I make a difference, and where I can move up the ladder. I need to narrow down my choices and make a good decision." *

Industry-wise, What's Hot? What's Not?
Industry Trends

Look through the information on various industries, companies and career possibilities you've collected so far, and identify those that will flourish, those that will languish. Think of these in the broader sense: technology, finance, education, engineering, consumer products, leisure, health and fitness, import/export, the environment, politics, entertainment, science. My personal opinion is that civil engineering will be a booming field in the future, because of the state of disrepair of the infrastructure nationwide. Natural disasters like Hurricane Katrina and wars have increased the need in construction and building trades nationally and abroad. This is good news for civil and structural engineers, as well as construction workers and the industries that support these professions. Not only these professions, but industries concerned with protecting and rebuilding the natural environment will work side by side to learn from our mistakes and understand the power of Mother Nature a little more.

Evaluate the general climate of the healthy industries that mesh with your interests, and identify those factors relevant to their success at this time. To do this, you need to get acquainted with your local librarian. You might be surprised at how friendly research librarians are. Rather than esoteric recluses, these people have been hired specifically to help people find whatever information they need. This can be anything from the Blue Book price of a used car to computer searches for stock market bargains. No question is too far out, or too simple, for them.

To begin with, they probably will direct you to the business and financial sections. They'll acquaint you with business and trade directories, periodical indexes, and abstracts and tell you what you can expect to find in them. They'll tell you about their "vertical files," that section of the library containing pamphlets and news clippings, which is probably your best bet for local information. They will also steer you toward any specialized business collections in other libraries in your area, such as at a university. These libraries are usually open to you as well, even if you don't have a card, as long as you use the material while you are there. Many of these have evening and weekend hours.

A good place to start, in any library, is with the *Reader's Guide to Periodical Literature*. In many libraries, the periodical index now runs on a computer, which is easier and faster. Look up general topics like "jobs." Many major magazines run general surveys on "Where the hot jobs are." Or look under specific industries. You will even find articles about specific companies.

Another good source for this kind of information is the U.S. Industrial Outlook, prepared by the U.S. Department of Labor. It gives key data on more than 350 different industries, such as general overviews, employment statistics, foreign competition, impact from technology, growth forecasts, career trends, and production and sales statistics. Each chapter gives a summary of the past year's performance, and positive and negative aspects that will affect the future. Standard and Poor's publishes similar material and includes financial comparisons of leading companies in each of the twenty-five major industries it profiles. All of this information is available to you online as well, so you have the option on the hard copy version or the online version.

     When Barbara returned for our next meeting, she had the information she needed to narrow down her fields and to make some informed choices. She had investigated several of the areas she had been excited about at the trade show. She checked the library's periodical guide for pertinent articles, and leafed through the Occupational Outlook Handbook and New Emerging Careers: Today, Tomorrow and in the 21st Century, by S. Norman Feingold and Norma Reno Miller. She separated the expanding areas from the contracting ones. She also came away with names of several successful companies in each expanding area. This investigation would also help her avoid interviews with companies in economic difficulty, and not waste valuable time exploring positions for which she was not qualified.

     Now write down what you imagine to be the ideal size, location, client mix, work environment, and project approach for your present career goals. Next, look for firms that closely fit that description. A common assumption is that you won't know many of these until you're hired. True, there is a lot you will have to assume or trust your judgment on, but there are resources that can provide you with some insight as to how an organization feels about its employees and attitudes within the organization that may influence you one way or another. Almost any company or organization of any size will have a website where you can get information about which they are, what their products and services are as well as information about open positions.

     Check out *The American Almanac of Jobs and Salaries*, particularly if you are a bit fuzzy about the industries you are interested in and are having a difficult time pinpointing the kinds of positions you might want to look at. This book gives you an opportunity to survey a variety of jobs in terms of specific tasks, salaries, and so on. The book contains close to 15,000 job descriptions, everything from rodeo clown to investment banker and a considerable variety of government positions. It is the most comprehensive guide in terms of job descriptions and what you can expect as starting salaries. Another excellent source of information is the Bureau of Labor Statistics at www.bls.gov.

Every year *Working Woman* magazine puts out an issue which features their list of the hundred best companies for women. I have referred clients to this list for years because it is a good starting point with companies that have already passed the screening of a magazine whose mission in part is to inform women on workplace issues. As far as I am concerned, the list is gender neutral, and both men and women have used the list successfully in their job search. Look at the list and see what criteria for selection *Working Woman* used, and then see what else the company was selected for. What companies sound interesting or like good prospects to you? Next, take a third look at the companies based on your interest areas and the industries you would like to target. Are any of those companies in your geographical preference area? If not, are there companies similar to the ones listed in your area? Do any of these companies bring up new areas you might want to explore further? Or is it a company you might want to put on your list of interesting career information to look over? You should make a file on your desktop or have a list of favorites that contains career information that you will look at often, add to, and replace with more current information. Remember, you are learning a process. How to take charge of your working life is something you will be involved with for quite a while, so you will want to start a "Career Library" file and refer to it often.

* After reading through half of New Emerging Careers: Today, Tomorrow and in the 21st Century, *Barbara began to see the validity of scrutinizing individual companies in terms of health and safety factors, insurance benefits, retirement benefits, stock options, early retirement packages, maternity leave, all of the issues she felt were going to be important to her as a working professional.*

Barbara had a lot of interests, and to help her narrow these down, she worked through the Values Exercise (Chapter 4). She found that her top priorities centered on creativity, independence, and working within her two disciplines. We now began to establish some criteria, including an opportunity to grow and an opportunity *for artistic expression. Barbara also felt a tremendous pull toward the sciences as well as art and wasn't quite sure which direction she favored. As we began to talk more about the kinds of organizations she wanted to work for, she focused first on artistic areas. If there was any way she could combine her two interests, that would just be frosting on the cake.* *

What Can I Do for You?
Researching Specific Positions

Now your personal desires and research begin to pay off. Your chances of hitting the bull's eye are far greater when you have a target than when you don't. Positions will jump out at you because you know what you have to market.

To expand your possibilities, look at career books in your particular area. VGA, for instance, publishes a whole series of *Opportunities in...* and *Careers in...* books. If you don't find material in your career field, ask the librarian if it is available from another library through the interlibrary loan program. Book searches on Amazon.com or similar websites under career information/job search yield extensive lists of the current and popular literature on these subjects. You will have your choice of titles to select from.

An important thing to remember as you are looking through all this information is that you are basically looking for two kinds of information: information about the industry and information about different positions within those industries. Let's use Health Care as an example of an industry. Information about this industry would tell what some of the trends in health care are, some ethical issues facing the industry, advances in the field, continued challenges, who some of the superstars are, as well as career ladders and organizational charts. Information on positions often focuses on the duties of a particular profession and the various places where that kind of profession is used. Let's use Nursing as our position within health care that we are researching. Nurses can work in hospitals, nursing homes, private duty, in education, as instructors, on construction sites, in research, in pharmaceutical companies, as consultants, as health journalists, as health promoters, in management, and so forth. My point is that once you know what it is a nurse does, you then have the opportunity to decide where and in what area you want to be a nurse and with what population. Information is power, and this kind of power in the workplace provides for high levels of confidence in your marketability and job security.

Ask to see *Standard Directory of Advertisers*, published by Standard Rate and Data Service, Inc. This guide indexes, by business category, all trade publications that accept paid advertising. Suppose you're interested in the travel industry but aren't aware of any job possibilities other than flight attendant or travel agent, neither of which appeals to you. In this guide, you'll find listings for several travel-related magazines, each directed to a different group of people in the travel business. You can get back issues of these magazines and explore the different kinds of jobs available in each area.

Two invaluable resources are *The Encyclopedia of Associations and Organizations* and *The American Trade and Professional Associations Directory*. These list thousands of organizations whose primary goals are to promote their particular field, and they are excellent sources of information. You can call the associations in your field and ask if there are local chapters and contact numbers. Find out if they have meetings. Ask for businesses that are affiliated with the organization. Ask about current trends.

Belonging to a professional organization is one of the best ways to get up-to-date literature and information on openings and trends in your field. I refer clients to these encyclopedias almost daily, and almost daily they tell me about the valuable information they received when they wrote and asked for directories. Most professional organizations have websites where you can access information that will be helpful in your career searches.

*   *"I'm getting a reputation for carrying the world's heaviest beach bag," Barbara laughed when we next met. "I've also found a lovely little espresso bar that serves great cappuccino and don't mind my hogging a table for hours with my laptop. Every now and then, someone even comes up and asks to look at some of the books and things I have scattered about."*

For her homework, I suggested she skim through High Tech Jobs for Non Tech Graduates, *because I felt Barbara' science background was still worthy of consideration and exploration. Other resources I suggested, such as* Professionals' Job Finder, *by Daniel Lauber, and* A Director of Information Resources in the U.S., Physical Sciences, Engineering, *were more closely related to her specific interests.*

I began to sense that the beach scene and cappuccino were wearing thin. "All I'm doing is looking at books, looking at books. I'm finding out more information, but I'm not sure where it's leading," Barbara grumbled.

"I think this will bring it into focus," I explained to her. "Start ranking the kinds of things you want in an organization and potential positions you might be interested in."

The list she returned to me was heavily weighted toward museums: art museums, museums of natural history, museums of space and technology, those kinds of things. Also included were medical publishers. I asked how she arrived at her list.

"I located most of it in A Directory of Information Resources in the U.S. *Here, I found places where I can combine my artistic talent with science," she replied." For instance, I'd never thought about medical illustration."*

Building on this, I suggested as her next task she look at what it takes to be a medical illustrator. We did a Google search and found enough information to carry Barbara and me into the next century but settled on the top ten and began to cull through the list. She was clearly showing more enthusiasm for this than I had seen with anything this far. I sensed we were getting close.

The library was again another source for her information. By now, she and the research librarian had become fast friends, and he helped her locate whatever was available. At our next meeting, Barbara's enthusiasm was still evident, but more focused, the information she had uncovered now creating its own momentum. She had already contacted a medical illustrator's organization in Los Angeles and gone to one of its meetings.

"It was wonderful," she said, her animation bubbling up again. "I found out about places where I could get additional training and certification. I also learned that one of the key

components to being a good medical illustrator is having a fine arts background, particularly working with the human form."

I could see she was really excited about this.

"When I was in school, I always entered work in the art shows. I did pretty well, too. Even Best of Show in a couple of them, and they were juried shows, too. And how about this? My best award was for a series of pen and ink drawings of the human figure!" She could hardly sit still. She also felt this was an excellent way for her to use her biology background. Her excitement carried her to the medical library at several of the local hospitals and the medical school at a nearby university.

"I've spent hours pouring over those books looking at the illustrations. I believe I've found my niche."

I asked her, "Why?"

"Because my heart starts beating faster when I look at this work, when I see the potential for helping people learn, and it feels like something I want to do with my life," she said. *

Begin compiling a list of names, addresses, telephone numbers, job titles and people within your chosen industry who can be important information resources. This will give you a framework for the final step conducting employer research.

Who Is Hiring, and How Do I Find Them?
Employer Research

Organizations, particularly private companies, spend thousands of dollars developing company literature with the expectation it will be read. Annual reports, recruiting materials, and business directories are excellent sources of information.

The easiest companies to research are those that are publicly owned, those that trade their shares on the various stock exchanges. The larger the company, the more information you will find. Look for geographical locations, names and profiles of company executives, and company addresses. Industry-specific directories are especially helpful here. This can be a fascinating but tedious process, so be prepared.

Look for background articles on the company and its products. In addition to the *Guide to Periodic Literature*, check for the *Business Periodicals Index, Predicasts F & S Index, Business Index, Infotrac,* and other online services, the *Wall Street Journal* and *New York Times* indexes. If your local newspaper has an index, you might check that, too.

Publicly owned and traded companies are required to publish an annual report, and these can be very informative, especially in describing new products and services, market share, corporate emphasis, and problems within the company or the industry. You'll find that this information is usually one of the menu picks on their company website. Even a quick study can get "the flavor" of a company, says David Batchelder, former chief strategies for corporate raider T. Boone Pickens and now head of his own investment firm. Madeline Aguirre (Chapter 8) learned through the annual report that the company she was going to interview with had recently purchased a food preparation company, key information that made a difference in her interview.

In addition, *Inc.* publishes an annual survey of 500 hottest private companies. *Business Week* publishes an annual guide to the 100 fastest-growing publicly held companies. *Hispanic Business Magazine* publishes lists of companies owned, operated, and involved in serving the worldwide Hispanic market. Trade magazines and newsletters are particularly helpful in providing leads on specific fields. Trade magazines like *Advertising Age, Philanthropy Today,* and *Publishers Weekly* also give excellent leads. Look for upcoming conventions and trade shows. It might be worthwhile to attend some seminars or meetings to make contacts. Always read the classified section of these magazines. They're a great source of information that's difficult to get anywhere else— like current salary ranges. Many, like *Editor & Publisher,* carry a "Help Wanted" section. Special issues can give you a real feel for areas that are often brushed over in regular issues.

Also, newspapers or popular and trade magazines publish information about contracts awarded to companies that may affect hiring. Examples might be: "Government awards contract to General Hospital to expand facilities." "Construction on new highway to begin next month." "Grand opening of new shopping mall is scheduled." This is again a test of how good a career consumer you have become. Headlines like this should jump out at you as employment opportunities first and new items second when your career radar is on.

If your company is local or regional in scope, the difficulty of finding public information increases. Ask the reference librarian what information they keep on local businesses. Some keep a good deal, others practically nothing. If you live in a large city, you are more likely to find local information than if you live in a smaller one. Most libraries will have an industrial directory published by their state, giving limited information on all manufacturers within their borders. You may also want to visit your newspaper office and see if they have an index, or if you can talk with their librarian.

Make sure you pay a visit to your local Chamber of Commerce and their website for information on local companies.

Your local Chamber of Commerce can be helpful. Many publish a magazine that includes stories about its members. Some have a person specifically charged with collecting and disseminating local economic information as well as current information on local businesses. This could well be your most informed source of information on local companies. Colleges and universities with business or economics departments are other good resources. They often publish information about local trends.

With local companies, try the direct approach—talk to someone there. With any company, large or small, public or private, begin by asking for information regarding the company's product or service. This also gives you an opportunity to see the work site. You might also ask for the name of the person in charge of the department you want to work in as well as the personnel director and any other key people. The receptionist often keeps their cards at the front desk. Better yet, ask for an organization chart, so that you have an idea of the number and size of various departments and who heads them. Ask if they have a newsletter. Larger companies, school systems, and institutions often have to keep the employees informed about other divisions. In-house newsletters are a good way to get a feel for the organizational atmosphere, as well as a sense of who the players are.

Before Barbara let her enthusiasm carry her away, I wanted to make sure she understood she still had options to explore.

"Medical illustration sounds like a very viable career move for you, but before you lock yourself in, why not get some more information on what you might do at a museum?" You spent a great deal of time and effort looking up information about museum work a few weeks back, and I want to make sure you have explored that as a career a little more before you leave it entirely.

"Back to the library," she shrugged with a sigh.

"Hold it." I swung my computer screen around and punched in the addresses for the local museums in town, had Barbara copy down pertinent contact information, and sent her on her way to conduct informational interviews with the Curator at each museum. *

Straight from the Horse's Mouth
Informational Interviews

For really down-and-dirty information, set up informational interviews—interviews designed to give you information, not a job. The distinction is very important. These are most productive if you prepare well.

Begin by seeking out the highest-ranking person doing the job that interests you. If you are aiming for a sales job, contact the top-ranking field sales executive in your preferred geographical area. These informational/networking interviews are the most effective way to open the doors of potential employers, because they put you in the right places at the right time to learn about potential job openings before they are ever publicized.

But beware. The sheer number of *What Color Is Your Parachute?* readers and other career changers has created a flood of information seekers. Predictably, employers and professionals have caught on and are making more careful judgments about whom to see and whom to turn away. Also, strangers do not want to be job exchange bureaus. They may know about job possibilities, but are reluctant to give this information to someone whom they have just met. If you are to get a referral, you will have to earn it.

* Barbara called the Curator of the local museum of natural history and met with her within the week. Her agenda was

clear. She wanted to know what positions were typically available at museums such as this, what those people did, and what their training was. She also asked to talk directly to people who held these positions.

The Curator was delighted in her interest because she seldom got requests for anything other than actual job interviews. They spent a fairly extensive morning touring the museum, going through the different departments, examining each position by job function and skill sets required.

Barbara's meeting was specifically fruitful. She was particularly interested in the artists who prepared the scenes, backdrops, and landscapes for the exhibits, as well as the people who were involved with exhibiting the artifacts of the museum. She talked with that particular cadre within the museum and found that they too had art backgrounds along with some science, particularly botany, geography, and anthropology.

"They showed me how they had to be able to draw their scenes to complement the native plant life that you see around the animals in the dioramas."

*She began to feel the same sort of fervor about exhibit preparation as she had about medical illustration. ***

One of the best resources for informational interviews for college grads is other alumni. Having graduated from the same school tends to create instant rapport. Even if you're targeting a job in finance and there's a graduate in your area who's a marketing executive, don't discount this person, since he or she may provide you with an introduction to someone in your targeted area. Many alumni associations publish directories, providing detailed information on the whereabouts, professionally and geographically, of graduates. Even if they don't have a published directory, alumni associations will sometimes provide this information. Many alumni associations have set up networks of alumni who are willing to talk to recent graduates about prospects with their organization or careers within their industry in general.

Keep in mind the informational interview is your show, so feel free to develop a list of prepared questions and take notes, or, if given permission, tape the session. I emphasize that one of the most significant ways to ensure a successful informational interview is the preparation beforehand. The questions you ask and the way you present yourself are extremely important. Some typical questions are:

- What kinds of entry-level jobs do you think are good training grounds for a person entering this field now?
- What are some of the criteria that a new entrant should use when considering a specific position?
- What education/degrees/training/licenses are needed?
- What are the trends and developments in the field that you see as affecting the career of someone just entering this occupation now?
- How much time do you estimate you spend each day in the various activities of your work?
- How do people in your position interact with others in your organization?
- What are some of the problems/decisions likely to face you in a day's time? What skills are required for handling them?
- What are the most satisfying parts of your work? Most frustrating?
- What are the constraints that affect you in your work? For example, financial, legal, supervisory, policy, consumer demand?
- Would you please trace your own career path?
- What professional organizations do you belong to, and what professional conferences do you attend to keep current in your field?
- Could you give me names, addresses, and telephone numbers of other people in this occupation who might be willing to talk with me about their careers as you have done?

You may find nonprofit organizations are more accessible and willing to take this kind of time. In the corporate world, people are not as likely to be able or willing to spend extended amounts of time with you. You might ask to take them to breakfast, lunch but some see this as an intrusion on their personal time. It's usually best to keep work-related issues at the work site. Wherever you meet, be sure your questions are very concise and very direct and recognize that you will probably spend less than an hour of their time getting your information.

Be sure to take a résumé with you, even if it is a multipurpose one. You can use it to simply and quickly share information about your background so that you can move on to the task of finding out about the interviewee's background and experience.

No question, this is one of the hardest parts of the job search, and one that takes time to fine-tune. Some of the things you should be looking for are: the organization's age, services, competitors within the industry as a whole, growth pattern, reputation, divisions and subsidiaries, location/length of time established there, size, number of employees, revenues, new projects, and number of locations. Of equal importance, try and get a feel for the corporate culture. Do the employees seem friendly with one another? Is there a congenial feel around the topic of their work? Does the staff demonstrate enthusiasm? Could you see yourself in an environment like this?

First Things First
Decision Time

It is now time for the question I finally pose to all my clients: What do you want to do first? You will have the option throughout your life to take on many different careers, to change careers, change positions, even change industries. But what are you going to do first, and where are you going to concentrate this job search? Now it's time to expand your investigations to specific organizations and job functions to develop an information network.

* *"I'm still having trouble making up my mind," Barbara admitted. "Both museum work and medical illustration are fascinating and fit my skills and lifestyle. I want them both." She sat back, tented her hands, and closed her eyes. She spoke slowly as she worked it through.*

"I believe I have the skills and background for a museum job right now. I'm excited about that, but I don't know if I want to do that for the rest of my life." She paused again. "I'll need more

training to become a medical illustrator. That's not impossible, but it will take a little while." She straightened herself. "I think I will begin by looking for jobs in museums as a scenic artist and exhibit technician."

Barbara started her search for a job as a museum exhibit technician by recontacting the artists at the natural history museum. They recommended professional publications and gave her a contact at the state professional organization. Before long, she had a list of four museums that met her criteria and had open positions. Her final choice was a small museum where she was given the greatest responsibility. It was located near a university, and she is now enrolled in classes leading to her certification as a medical illustrator. Then it will be decision time all over again. *

Researching the job market may seem tedious, but it is essential and effective. As with any learning curve, it begins slowly, but the momentum builds and suddenly you achieve the Velcro effect. You become a "career consumer," choosing wisely and efficiently. To achieve this goal, keep in mind it takes work, diligence, commitment, a willingness to ask for help, time, and above all, patience. The reward is a truly satisfying career chosen from among many. In this instance, your choice will be made after creating a solid knowledge base about yourself and what kind of job market you want to be in. As you grow in experience and adult responsibility, you will make different choices about your work and the role it will play in your life. I encourage you to consistently refer to the file you have created with your favorite websites and career information. The way to stay strong and vibrant in the job market is to stay informed and ahead of the curve. Be able to forecast the changes before they happen and make the adjustments to your career before they are forced on you by circumstance. This knowledge and how you use it produce the ultimate job security.

THE PROFESSIONAL SELF MODEL
A THREE-STEP PROCESS

The Professional Self is an attitude, created through knowledge, focused through research and packaged to sell.

STEP 1
PERSONAL ASSESSMENT

Explore your skills, interests, work values, and personality style to know yourself and what you are capable of.

STEP 2
EXPLORING & RESEARCHING THE JOB MARKET

Learn to identify global and national issues that point to expanding and contracting markets, identify expanding industries in your fields of interest, specific organizations in those industries, and positions you can actually apply for.

STEP 3
DEVELOPING YOUR MARKETING TOOLS

Learn how to create dynamite résumés, stand out in interviews, and negotiate strategies to get the most out of the job. Discover how to support these with correspondence that sells. Learn how to generate industry-specific materials that sell your ability.

Based on: Maestas, Lily, M.S.W., and Lorelei Snyder. *Unlimited Options: Career Strategies to Last a Lifetime,Goleta CA 93117.* Prosperity Press, 1996.

- Create "value-adding" correspondence that gets you noticed and remembered.

- Dress up your raw data to showcase a star performer.

- Develop industry-specific and position-targeted résumés.

- Present yourself as a self-confident candidate at any interview.

- Practice the steps for successful negotiation.

- Feel the power of your Professional Self.

Part III

Developing Your Marketing Tools

7   Correspondence That Sells
Whom to Write to—Why, When, and How

"As you progress through this job search, remember words create a thousand pictures."

Sooner or later, you are gong to have to write to your prospective employers. Effective letters are pivotal job marketing tools. The written message gives the potential employer an insight into how you communicate, organize, and present your thoughts and, quite frankly, how well you write. Every job search takes on a personality of its own and requires its own specific correspondence. You know you can't get away from cover letters and thank-you notes, but there are other pieces of correspondence you may overlook, such as:

- Clarification letters
- Acceptance/rejection letters
- Query letters
- Questionnaires
- Industry-specific materials

Cover Letters

A cover letter with your résumé is obligatory. Whether your letter gets read or not, the message you send is that you know what the appropriate procedure is for a résumé. Think of it as being similar to serving someone a piece of cake. Not everyone eats the frosting, but everyone likes to see it. Sending a résumé without a cover letter is like serving someone a piece of cake without the frosting.

Your cover letter is a sales presentation. It's your initial opportunity to set the stage for your résumé, and to tune the employer in to why you should be considered. It needs to catch the reader's attention, persuade him or her of your value, and convince him or her to act. It is a brief, well-written introduction to your résumé.

141

I always advise following the 1–2–1 approach. That is, your cover letter should consist of three paragraphs, the first about one inch long, or no more than six typed lines; the second about two inches; and the third no longer than one inch, or a total of about twenty-four typed lines. This forces you to write short, concise letters. Your statements must be clear, definitive, and to the point.

The basic message in your first paragraph is an introduction. You want to let the reader know who you are and why he or she is being contacted. Try to be more creative than "Regarding your ad for an administrative assistant," but also avoid the other extreme such as: "I am a dynamic go-getter seeking a high-profile position with a fast-growing organization." You might look at something like, "After a successful and rewarding five years in the computer industry, I have now set my sights on entering the accounting field." Or for the recent grad, "As a graduating senior from Emerson State University with a Bachelor's degree in Computer Graphics, I am currently looking for positions in animation." You let them know who you are and what you want. If possible, let them know you are responding to a specific vacancy announcement and where you encountered it. If this position was brought to your attention through personal or professional contacts, this is the paragraph in your cover letter where you should mention that contact. It is not necessary to go into great detail about who this person is and how you know him or her. The point is to let your reader know that this was a personal referral; however, this first paragraph and the whole letter, for that matter, is about you, so be brief in your mention of other people.

The second paragraph is what I call the "meat and potatoes section." The information does not reiterate your résumé but rather enhances it and encourages the reader to turn to it. You may want to expand on your reasons for pursuing this particular organization or share some bit of information you know about the company. Try to express yourself in no more than twelve typed lines. You might choose three aspects of your work experience, achievements, or abilities that demonstrate how well-suited you are for the job, and bullet them for emphasis. If you are a little shy of the job qualifications, but you have comparable experience, here is the place to emphasize it.

The third paragraph is the "action and closing." Tell them what you are planning to do next, but try to avoid the, "I look forward to hearing from you" business. Request an application. Suggest a meeting time. You might try something like: "I'll contact you in a week to discuss employment opportunities," or "I look forward to an opportunity to discuss with you further my qualifications and interest in this position." Be sure to let them now how to reach you and when it's easiest. Letting them know when you will be available for employment is also something important to mention.

Again, brevity and clarity are the order of the day. Here is an example of the 1–2–1 approach in action.

Lucille had known since she was eight years old that she wanted to live in New Mexico. That was the first summer her grandparents included her on their annual trek to the American Southwest. She looked forward to their weekly excursions onto the Indian reservations where her grandfather volunteered at the medical clinic and her grandmother took her on walks with the tribal women to explore cave dwellings and ruins.
Later, Lucille returned to New Mexico to attend college, where she majored in journalism and Native American studies. In her senior year, she spent a semester at the Los Angeles Times on an internship.
When she graduated, she was determined to remain in New Mexico and to work with the Bureau of Indian Affairs. Here is the cover letter she included with her résumé when she applied for a job she unearthed while researching a story during her internship.
*

Dear Ms. Miller:

As a recent graduate from the University of New Mexico with a double major in Journalism and Native American Studies, I am seeking a position that will utilize my academic and practical experience. I believe the position you mentioned in the **Los Angeles Times** *10/22/05 article provides for such an opportunity.*

As my résumé indicates, I have held a variety of positions writing for the university newspaper as well as professional internship experience with the **Los Angeles Times.** *My interest in working with the Bureau of Indian Affairs and specifically Corporate Communications came after tracking a story for the* **LA Times** *in which you highlighted the work being done by your agency in linking major corporations with Native American tribes in the preservation of historical artifacts. I believe my credentials will be of interest to you.*

I have enclosed a copy of my résumé for your review as well as several articles I wrote while working on the university paper. I look forward to the possibility of employment with you. I will call your office on Monday. I would like to schedule a meeting with you on Thursday or Friday of next week, if that would be convenient. I look forward to our time together.

Sincerely,

Lucille Anderson
Enclosure

If possible, your cover letter should be addressed to someone, not just to a title or an office. It is too easy for your letter and any other material you send with it to end up in the round file unread if you do not mail it directly to someone by name. This is where your employer research pays off. You may be able to get the proper person simply by calling the company and asking for the name of the personnel manager. If you are stuck with responding to a box number, avoid the standard "Dear Sir:" and try something more neutral, such as "Hello!" or "Good Morning!"

The correspondence that accompanies a job search will take place in a variety of ways. The most typical will be through emails and electronic correspondence; however, it is important to maintain a paper trail or record of your interaction with potential employers as part of an organized job search. This chapter is not so much about how you send the correspondence but rather the different types of correspondence you should be aware of when engaging in an active job search.

Thank-You Letters

You write thank-you letters because it is the right thing to do. Think about it. You have asked someone to fill out a questionnaire you developed. Perhaps you conducted an informational interview with him or her and the person gave you the name of a friend in another company to contact. You asked someone to write you a letter of recommendation or to serve as a reference during your job search. You had an especially good interview experience with a personnel director and want to make contact again and express continued interest in the position. In each case, someone has given you something, and it is only right that you express gratitude for their intervention on your behalf.

Second, you write thank-you letters because they are effective marketing pieces. Studies show that the highest correlation between those looking for work and those who get job offers is the thank-you letter. What's more, nurturing the relationship may keep your contact interested in aiding your job search through leads, contacts, and maybe even an offer down the road. One of the major vehicles for conducting a successful job search is networking. An important way to make sure networking happens is through the liberal use of thank-you letters. It is important to build bridges and keep in touch. Letting people know you appreciate their efforts on your behalf makes them feel the time they took out of their day was worthwhile. Being told you are appreciative is a major reason for people to continue to take an active interest in your success.

Thank-you notes are most often short and handwritten, if you're writing is legible, although emailed thank-you notes are now common. I still think that a handwritten thank-you note on nice stationery sent through the mail leaves a valuable impression. An effective thank you can be as simple as this:

Dear Mr. Powell:

I would like to take a minute of your time to thank you for the interview for the graphic design position with your firm this past Monday. As a result of our discussion, I am more certain than ever that there is a place for me at Melmen Advertising.

Sincerely,

Barbara Bailey

Thank-you letters should recall for the receiver his or her part in your job search, and they require careful thought and preparation. This may dictate a longer, more detailed letter.

* When Leigh composed her thank-you letter for a job interview, it took a full four hours, in addition to the research it refers to. Although somewhat longer than usual, it did the trick. Upper management was impressed with the effort that went into it, and decided to take a chance on her, even though she had no direct experience in sales. *

Dear Mr. Ware:

Thank you for the extensive time you took with me last week. I thoroughly enjoyed the morning. I believe working with your company would be an exciting and rewarding challenge.

Since our meeting, I have discussed the leasing business here in Santa Barbara with some of my Chamber of Commerce contacts. Their comments confirm that there is definitely an expanding market for this business, but they also noted that the competition is keen. Rates vary but little, and approvals can take as little as one day. Where approvals are difficult to get, the circumstance is usually one of a slow-pay history, and I wonder how your company treats such situations?

Although many of the existing leasing companies provide sales training programs for their customers such as you described, few do it on a regular, consistent basis. Indeed, when I asked, "What would create company loyalty for you?" the answer was unanimously "Service!" I believe you have a winner there. Other comments included, "My customer gets quick approval, and I get quick payment."

If your sales expectations are accurate, I can see clearly they will not be achievable without a great deal of dedicated hard work, with an astute eye toward prompt and good service. I believe I can deliver that.

I would look forward to spending two weeks with you learning the business and the territory. During that time I would expect to identify at least ten key manufacturing areas for initial pursuit. I am confident that by then I will be well qualified to "solo."

Yours very truly,

Leigh Kilbourne

Your appreciation is what should be the central theme of any thank-you letter. If you can, it is also a good idea to let the person know the outcome of the job search and the part he or she played in making it successful. If the person you were referred to in another company eventually offered you a position, tell him or her that. If his or her responses on the questionnaire provided you with added insight into a particular industry, tell them so. If your interview went well and there were one or two highlights that you can recall, mention them. But first and foremost, you are writing to say thank you for taking the time to be part of something that was very important to you.

* When one of her references gave her a personal referral, Amanda followed up with great results. Here's what she wrote: *

Dear Esther:

Thank you so much for your wonderful letter of recommendation. Your comments were very kind and addressed some of my most pertinent work-related experience. This job search has certainly been exciting and filled with unexpected surprises. The most memorable is your referral to your sorority sister at Athens Industries. As a result of that referral and my follow-up, I have been offered an engineering position with Athens, one that I think I am going to accept.

Your active participation in my job search has made a tremendous difference. In the future, I hope to be able to model your generous example with another "talented young professional" who may one day seek my assistance.

Thank you once again for your efforts.

Sincerely,
Amanda Madison

Clarification Letters

Cover letters and thank-you letters are musts, but there are other opportunities when a good letter will make a difference.

The clarification letter is most often used by someone moving up or laterally within the same organization or by someone who has taken on a work assignment for a limited time. Usually, these kinds of work assignments involve extra compensation for the additional work responsibilities. Salary negotiations and upgrading of benefits packages also make clarification letters necessary.

The letter provides written documentation of the changes you have agreed to make as you understand them. If there is confusion between you and your employer regarding these changes, the clarification letter usually identifies them early and avoids misunderstandings down the road. Differing recollections or information that does not get passed on to a new supervisor can be devastating.

* JoAnn had worked as a social worker at Community Hospital for seven years. During that time, she developed particular expertise in the area of discharge planning for elderly stroke patients. The steady increase in the numbers of these patients finally demanded a reorganization of the department without, of course, increasing staff. The hospital administration asked Joan to supervise the project. She was excited by the opportunity to "see that it gets done right."

In her acceptance letter, she wanted to make it clear that this temporary work assignment would require her to relinquish some of her current responsibilities, but that she expected to resume her original position when it was finished. The letter Joan wrote outlined the parameters of the agreement with time lines, salary adjustments, and position title changes. There was very little left to the imagination, which is exactly what Joan wanted. *

Dear Mr. Baldwin:

I am excited about the opportunity to develop and implement a new discharge planning component. I appreciate your confidence in me. To be sure I am clear regarding our discussion last week; I would like to outline for both of us my understanding regarding this reorganization and the part I will play.

1. *On March 16, I will assume the responsibility of Project Manager for the reorganization of the Discharge Planning Unit of the Social Work Service at the hospital. The project is estimated to last six months and will include the completion of the following tasks:*

   A. *Evaluation of all positions within the component, including appropriate recommendations for reclassification and salary adjustments.*

   B. *Review of the current budget with recommendations regarding effective use of resources.*

   C. *Review and modification of the current referral system to accommodate the increase in elderly discharge planning assignments. The change in procedure will reflect the need for increased interaction with geriatric referral sources within the Greater Los Angeles area.*

   D. *In an effort to minimize disruption of services and promote cooperation, weekly updates and input from the staff will be crucial. A list of the scheduled meetings for the next three months is attached.*

2.   *As a result of this project, I will be relieved of my caseload assignments effective immediately. Said responsibilities will be reinstated upon completion of the project. In order to complete this project in a timely manner, you have agreed to provide me with two additional support staff personnel to handle the increase in paperwork and ensure proper documentation of procedures.*

3.   *During the next six months, my salary will reflect a thousand dollars a month increase, which will terminate at the completion of this project. My title will be Project Manager, and I will report directly to Harriet Briggs, Chief Administrative Officer of the hospital. The final report will be due three weeks after completion of the project and will be submitted directly to the Board of Directors of the hospital.*

I am looking forward to the challenge this opportunity represents and am confident the resulting recommendations will make a tremendous difference in the discharge planning, thus ensuring higher quality services to our patients. I am delighted to have this opportunity and would like to thank you again for the assignment.

If you have any questions regarding the above outline, please talk with me at your earliest convenience.

Sincerely,

JoAnn Tajima, MSW

Keep in mind, it is your best interest to take the initiative and outline for your employer what you see the changes will be in your relationship. Don't wait until the information is presented to you. If it is incorrect, you are then put in the awkward position of having to correct your boss, whereas, if you outline the changes first, you present yourself as a conscientious employee attempting to avoid conflict.

Acceptance/Rejection or Counteroffer Letters

Once you are in a position to write an acceptance/rejection or a counteroffer letter, you know all your hard work has paid off. Congratulations! You hold in your hand a job description and title, salary offer, and a benefits package, and your reply is eagerly awaited.

It's always best to give yourself a few days to think it over, even if you are sure that you will accept the position. Why? Most important for me is the opportunity to bask in the glow of success. Very seldom do we have an opportunity to feel this good about something and I think you should take advantage of this moment purely for its own sake!

A more down-to-earth reason is to allow time to really review the job responsibilities, travel requirements, salary, and benefits to see what you are actually buying into.

* In some cases it's easy. After conducting a thorough job search in a number of industries, Bill, a laboratory chemist, was delighted when he was offered a position requiring the use of his scientific training to help develop solutions to world hunger. He felt his personal values were closely aligned with those of the organization and looked forward to the "team project" approach exhibited in the laboratory. In accepting the position, he wanted to give the employer some indication of his enthusiasm for the organization. *

Dear Mr. Silverman:

This is a follow-up to our conversation last Friday regarding the position as Food Chemist for Allied Biotechnology. After reviewing the information you sent over by messenger, I am pleased to accept your offer of employment starting October 15.

Working to provide alternative food sources for drought-stricken areas is, for me, an excellent way to use my scientific training and provide possible solutions for international hunger problems. Quite frankly, I can't think of a better way to put my education and energy to use than in looking for potential food sources for the world's hungry. I am looking forward to my association with the other chemists I met while on the plant tour last week as they seemed to share my enthusiasm for this project.

I am returning your copy of the signed contract. I will wait for your orientation materials to be sent at a later date. I look forward to a productive and satisfying relationship with Allied Biotech.

Sincerely,
William Rojas

* On the other hand, Amanda was faced with tactfully rejecting an offer from a hospital that had shown obvious interest and enthusiasm for her. During her job search, she had narrowed her industries of interest to health care and insurance. At this juncture, she had received two offers, one in each field, both attractive. However, in her research she learned of a great deal of internal strife in the department in which she would work at the hospital, resulting in high turnover. Although she liked Valley Hospital and thought that some day she might like to work there, she was not interested in accepting this current offer. Here's how she handled it: *

Dear Ms. Evans:

After careful consideration of your offer of employment as an accountant, I have decided not to accept at this time. This has been a difficult decision on my part as you presented some interesting professional challenges. However, an offer from another industry appears to more closely match my career needs at this point.

I continue to hold Valley Hospital in high regard and would consider employment with you should the right opportunity present itself at a later date. Thank you for the time you spent with me during this interview process, and I wish you the best of luck.

Sincerely,

Amanda Forrest, CPA

Some offers are not so simple. You may want to negotiate for a different benefits package, or clarify your responsibilities, or make a counter proposal. The time to do this is before you sign a contract, not afterward. Most employers will want to hurry the acceptance process along since negotiating with you is not seen as in their best interests. Remember that their main objective is to hire the best employee for the least amount of money.

* After reviewing the job offer, Andy was not quite satisfied, so he made a counteroffer. Here is his letter: *

Dear Mr. Sandstrom:

I was excited to receive your offer of employment last week. The thought of working for Johnson Industries in San Diego is appealing, and I look forward to a positive resolution to some of the disparities we discussed in our phone conversation last week.

I want to assure you that I am very interested in the position and the job activities, even though the particulars of employment have yet to be agreed upon. In an effort to move in that direction, I am proposing the following changes in your salary and benefits offer.

1. *I would like to propose that we share the relocation costs equally and forgo for this year your funding of my membership in the American Public Health Association. My membership is current, and renewal will not be necessary until a year from now. The money you have allocated to cover that expenditure could be used to cover your portion of the moving expenses.*

2. *I understand that the salary you quoted is non-negotiable. I would like to suggest that we shorten the time before my first performance review to six months as opposed to a year. In that time, I am confident that you will have had a chance to observe my work, and we can discuss salary options at that time.*

If these two revisions in your proposal meet with your approval, I see no reason for me to delay accepting your offer of employment. I look forward to hearing from you.

Sincerely,

Andrew Miller

*Take note that in the counteroffer Andy clearly states his desire to accept the job, but the conditions of employment are not quite what he had in mind. In both of his proposals, he mentions what he wants changed and offers reasonable alternatives. He becomes part of the solution as opposed to just presenting the company with a problem. It presents a positive, problem-solving, and interactive approach to the situation rather than a defensive one. ***

Query Letters

Query letters are useful if you are conducting an out-of-the area job search or are interested in a particular aspect of an industry; they can also be used as a prelude to an informational interview. Your query letter is one step in the process of matching what you discovered from your personal assessment with what is available in the market place. Your primary purpose is to get your contacts to give you information and advice, refer you to others, and remember you. Query letters are constructed to be non-threatening to the reader and demonstrate a genuine desire to gather information only. If it comes across as a disguised attempt to gain employment or secure a job interview, you blew it.

Key things to remember here: Make sure you include an estimate of the amount of time you think the interview will take, when you will contact them for an appointment and specifics as to the nature of the interview.

*Jonathan (Chapter 2) sent out the following letter to fifteen people in the entertainment and music industry. Out of those, three, or 20 percent, agreed to speak with him. ***

Dear Mr. Marquez:

After a significant amount of research into the music and entertainment industry, I have selected you as one of the fifteen people whose opinion I am interested in obtaining. I am currently working with a career counselor exploring alternative career options for myself. Having entered the insurance industry as an actuary immediately upon graduation from college, I am now ready to move into my next career and am looking for ways to combine my professional experience with my lifelong interest in music.

I am seriously considering making a career change into this industry. As this is a major departure for me, I am fully aware that it will require additional education and training on my part. Before I make that commitment, I want to know from those who know best the variety of positions available within the industry for someone with my academic and professional qualifications. With this information, I will be able to construct an efficient and effective plan of action.

I am aware that pressures on your time are great, but I would appreciate it if you would schedule just one-half hour with me to share your expertise and personal observations on this matter. The information I gather will help me to better focus my efforts.

I appreciate your consideration of my request and will call you next week to discuss a convenient time for you. Thank you in advance for your help. I look forward to talking with you.

Sincerely,

Jonathan Banks

In reference to this particular letter, I would like to mention that it was one of these contacts that eventually led Jonathan to his new position. One of the music industry lawyers he had initially contacted remembered him when he had a "free spirited" musician who needed tending. He contacted Jonathan, gave him the referral, and the rest, as they say, is history.

Questionnaire

A questionnaire allows you to ask standardized questions and gather consistent information from a variety of sources without having to interview each of the participants directly.

This is an extremely useful tool if you keep clear about your objective, which is to gather information that will help you narrow and focus your job search. In designing your questionnaire, be brief. It is better to design yes/no, or multiple choice questions. Essay questions are time consuming, and few people are willing to take the time to write down lots of information. More likely, they will put it aside in a "To Do Later" file, and you know what happens to that. You can include a request for comments after some of your questions, but only as an option. Your questionnaire should take no more than ten minutes to fill out. Less than five is even better. Keep the length to no more than two pages.

The content of the questions is entirely up to you and should be based on the kind of information you need. Make sure to include a cover letter with your questionnaire. Need we say it's important to follow up all replies with a thank-you letter?

* For as long as she could remember, Janice had spent her summers either attending or working at summer camps, and now, as she approached graduation, she wanted to continue in that field.

One of our annual campus events is a Camp Day. Directors from over fifty summer camps come to interview students for summer counselor and activity coordinator positions. I encouraged Janice to develop a questionnaire to hand out to the participating directors to fill out and return to her at the end of the day. In the questionnaire, she asked about their own career paths, educational training, and work experience that gave them the credentials needed for a director's position.

By and large, people like to talk about their careers and how they got there. It makes a good impression when someone wants to learn from their experiences, and it makes them more likely to take an interest in answering and returning the survey. In a relatively short time, not only was Janice able to get information from a large number of people in positions exactly like the one she herself wanted, she also made initial contact with these directors in a very positive way. *

CAMP DIRECTOR INFORMATION QUESTIONNAIRE

Hi! My name is Janice Maderios, and I am a student here at UCSB. I have been considering a career as a Camp Director of outdoor and/or summer camps. At our career center, I found information for this type of job. I am hoping that your knowledge and experience can give me personal knowledge and insight. Please take just five minutes to answer the following questions. Thank you.

1)   How did you first get involved in camps and/or recreation?
- ☐ As a counselor
- ☐ As a participant
- ☐ Transferred from a related field
- ☐ Other _____

2)   What specifics helped you to get this job?
- ☐ Licenses
- ☐ Internships
- ☐ Volunteer work
- ☐ Special classes
- ☐ Former positions
- ☐ Other _____

3)   How many hours a week do you spend at this position? Could you break these hours down into specific categories? (bookkeeping, publicity, hiring personnel, supervision, etc.)

4)   What future opportunities could this job open up for you? (Various other jobs, different fields, higher education)

5)   What is your educational background in terms of school, degree, studies, etc.?

6)   Please describe your camp.
        Camper Demographics _____
        Camper Population _____ Staff_____
        Average Session _____ Setting _____
        Activities
        ☐ Swimming   ☐ Tennis   ☐ Horseback riding
        ☐ Crafts   ☐ Dancing   ☐ Rifle range
        ☐ Campfires   ☐ Camping   ☐ Canoeing
        ☐ Sailing   ☐ Religious   ☐ Specialized skills
        ☐ Other (please specify) _____

7)   What professional associations do you belong to and why?

8)   May I write/contact you if I have further questions?
Y_____ N_____
Name _____
Title _____
Camp _____
Address _____
        _____
Email_____

9) Is there someone else you know in this field that I might benefit from speaking with?
        Name_____
        Contact Information:

Thank you for your time. Your investment in my future is very much appreciated!

Just recently, I had another student in my class use a similar questionnaire when she was invited to attend a conference of health educators working at college health centers. She had worked as a peer substance abuse educator as a student and was now interested in getting some full-time work experience before she applied to graduate school in Public Health. She handed out twenty-five questionnaires at the beginning of the conference. Two days later, she had made countless friends among the health educators, had lots of information and two invitations to apply for full-time positions that were open at other universities! It really does work. It takes a little effort and a bit of risk to put yourself out there, but I have seen this tool be highly effective in making that first impression and gathering initial information for your job search.

Industry-Specific Materials

Some industries require very specific documentation of your work. Journalists, writers, editors, and those involved with the written word will need to submit writing samples. When a friend of mine wanted to become a news reporter, she submitted clippings of published articles she had written for a community theater group and as public relations chair for the local League of Women Voters. Architects, graphic designers, artists, and people involved in advertising will usually have to submit a portfolio of their work. Those in the broadcast industries will need to submit tapes.

How do you gather this kind of material if you are still in the process of job changing or have never worked in the industry? Take a look around you. Where can you get the experience you need for your new career on an unpaid basis? What needs doing in your favorite charity? What about your church? Internships and volunteer work not only provide you with the means for creating this material, they will help you establish a track record in your new profession.

The rule of first impressions applies to your portfolio as well as your appearance. Include only your best work, presented in the most professional format you can create.

As you progress through this job search, remember words create a thousand pictures. The written word calls attention to your assets, recalls your uniqueness, reiterates your strengths, and demands a response. It makes people feel good about knowing you. Don't neglect it. Make your words a well-used power tool on your job-search workbench.

8   Creating a Convincing Résumé
Use Your Database to Repackage Yourself

"As you progress through this job search, remember words create a thousand pictures."

The job of a résumé is to get you interviews. A winning résumé package gives the employer a basic understanding of your qualifications for the job, a curiosity about who you are, and a desire to know more about you. It inspires the employer to invite you for an interview.

A good résumé:
- Attracts attention.
- Creates interest.
- Describes accomplishments.
- Provokes action (interviews).

It should:
- Emphasize pertinent data.
- Communicate job-related skills.
- Create the desired image.

A good résumé has:
- A clearly stated Career Objective.
- A skills listing directly related to the career objective.
- A listing of pertinent work and experience history.
- A listing of education and training.

For a career changer, the key is to identify what you want to move to, and then create a résumé that points in that direction. You may need to spend some time identifying your interests, skills, and experiences, and finding a good match for them in the new workplace.

* After three years on the fast track with a major retailer, Ellen Fairchild was ready to toss it away in favor of a new career,

163

but she felt locked in, trapped. The feeling is not unusual. Looking at her résumé, her experience, training, and accomplishments pointed in one direction, and she wanted to go in another.

"Way back in my freshman year, I stopped in at the college radio station. I'd never been in a radio station before, but Bingo!" Her fists exploded. "I thought, 'Wow! This is for me.' There was a sign up sheet for volunteers, and from then on I was hooked."

She spent all her spare time at the station, always eager for another experience. Now at this current crossroad, her goal was to become an on-air radio personality.

"Why didn't you go into radio right out of college?" I asked.

"It seemed too frivolous," she told me. "Everyone was so sure I'd be such a terrific manager, it seemed silly not to take advantage of the retail opportunity I had." She paused a moment. "Whenever I mentioned my radio work, everyone reacted like it was some kind of a hobby thing." She paused again, reflecting. "It is a risky business, and I wasn't confident enough about myself and my capabilities at graduation to even mention it as a career possibility." But after learning the retail business, Ellie also learned she had no passion for it. She began thinking more seriously about a radio career as she became more secure with herself.

"I know I'm good at management," she acknowledged and then added pragmatically, "I can always come back to it. Now I want to do what I have always felt, deep down inside, I should have done in the first place. I'm ready to try something risky, something adventurous, and I need to do it while I still have the guts to go for it."

Ellie was a realist. She recognized she had an uphill battle to convince someone to take a chance on a newcomer. *

As I begin to work on résumés with my clients, I notice they often stop with just a description of their previous job responsibilities. My advice is to carry that two steps further, telling the employer what skills you feel the experience required and what was the result of your having had the experience, what it accomplished. Noted career author Howard Figler points out that you must make connections between what you have done in the past and what you can do in the future. Accomplishments can be either personal or professional. If you had a position in sales and you were named top volume winner for the year, say so. Skills and accomplishments can also be on a personal or volunteer level.

The job of editing will come later, but for now you should concentrate on getting familiar with all your experiences and dissecting them into responsibilities, skills, and accomplishments. In the final résumé, this section will change as your Career Objective changes, but for now you are developing a bank of experiences you will be able to rearrange as the need arises.

Write everything down so you can examine each activity in detail. One of the greatest benefits of getting your credentials down on paper is that it helps to pinpoint how they can be improved. In time, you'll be able to pick each one of your activities apart in minute detail and describe in just a few short phrases the pertinent parts of each activity.

If you are changing fields entirely, the résumé becomes one of your most important job search tools. It is your calling card, your first impression, your initial attempt to capture the attention of a prospective employer. It is a positioning statement, a profile of who you are and why you're qualified for the job you want, a concise means of introducing yourself to a potential employer. One way of looking at your résumé is to think of it as a piece of direct-mail advertising—and the product is you. As in any effective direct-mail piece, it should be attractive in appearance, provocative in content, and positive in approach. The emphasis is always on what the product (you) has done and is capable of doing. Its purpose is to convince the employer that you have enough of the necessary skills and experience to warrant an interview.

The next step is to organize the various elements that make for an effective résumé and create a working draft. Start with the basic components. Since no two résumés should be the same, you should use the information you develop as you would an à la carte menu, choosing those that best suit the particular needs of each specific position. Look carefully at the information you've developed, and choose the skills, interests, and job-related experiences that apply to this particular job. These are the only ones you'll want to incorporate into your résumé.

I am always puzzled when people send out the same résumé for a variety of positions and then are disappointed and even angry because no one responds. It is not uncommon for successful job changers to prepare four or five different résumés, all having basically the same information, but organized and presented differently for each Career Objective.

We went back over Ellie's radio experience. Throughout her college years, Ellie had written copy, conducted interviews, and hosted an on-air talk show. We began to outline each of her jobs during the ten to fifteen hours a week she routinely spent as an intern at the station. We broke each of those positions down according to responsibilities, skills, and accomplishments. As she began to get a better feel for her assets, she began to validate for herself that this change was truly the direction she wanted to go. This process encouraged her decision to make her move now and gave her the self-confidence she needed to meet the natural resistance she experienced from her family and friends who thought she had lost her mind.

*We reviewed her academic work, looking for lab classes that provided her with hands-on experience, with opportunities to translate theory into practice. "Don't overlook the significance of the research work you did for your senior thesis, or the work you did on your media images research project," I urged. All these experiences provided valuable skills and demonstrated experience in a variety of areas that she then translated into qualifications for the new job. ***

For your first draft, start at the top of the page and list your name, address, and telephone number, where it's easy for the employer to see. This information is not always as obvious as it seems.

Take your name, for instance. Maybe you think this is only a cosmetic thing, but I believe what you call yourself and how others refer to you are very important in establishing the Professional Self you want to project. What you're trying to do is enhance that image. If you're thinking of a job at a bank, you'll want to present yourself as business-like, and William V. Smith, Jr., would be appropriate. If the job is in construction, Bill Smith will probably work just fine. And if you're looking at a job with a recreation department, Chip Smith makes you sound warm and friendly. Women looking for professional positions often find the use of initials helpful in overcoming gender bias. As you develop your own résumé, ask yourself: Does the way I present my name match the company and the position I'm applying for?

*Ellie looked at the job description she had brought from a small radio station in Santa Cruz, California. E. B. Fairchild had been the most appropriate signature for her management position. It was helpful in getting her ideas and recommendations reviewed in a neutral environment. In this case, however, she felt her nickname, Ellie, gave the right amount of informality for an on-air radio position. *

Now think about your telephone number. Most personnel people prefer to work normal business hours. Especially when entry-level positions are at stake, they are not likely to stay after five o'clock trying to reach you. Some research suggests the standard number of calls to a potential employee is three, and then they give up and go on to the next on the list. Make sure you have a professionally appropriate message on your answering machine as well as your cell phone. Listing your email address is also standard for résumés.

Ambitious Professional Wants Good Title
Career Objectives

The next step is to develop a Career Objective. This is important as much for your sake as for your employer. Your Career Objective is your hypothesis. You are stating to the employer: "This is what I want to do." It gives your résumé a focus. It also focuses you. With a clear objective, you can target your search toward a specific job market. It will also help you organize your entire job search into a coherent and manageable whole.

Ellie made her Career Objective specific: An entry-level position as an On-Air Personality providing an opportunity to utilize proven communication and organizational skills.

We talked about the possibility of Ellie seeking technical work or management responsibilities at the radio station, areas where she unquestionably had credentials, but she was adamant— she wanted on-air experience, and that was what she was going for.

*"An on-air personality is anonymous," she explained, somewhat embarrassed. "I've always felt I've traded on my looks. It's important to me to be successful on my own, without people knowing what I look like." **

Your career objective can be flexible. Employers want to know that you want what they want. Under the best circumstances, a job description or position vacancy notice will give you a specific job title to list. This creates a framework for both you and the employer, and allows the option of selecting only those experiences that reflect your abilities in relation to that particular objective. Be specific about the kind of job you are looking for, or what skills you want to use, with what kind or type of organization, and, if it's important, where in the country.

Your career objective should give the employer some general career categories from which to evaluate the information on your résumé. This is especially important if you are not responding to a specific position. Let's say, for example, a personnel director has two résumés in front of her, one without, one with a Career Objective. What is the personnel director supposed to do with the information on the first résumé? Since the résumé has not stated what the person is looking for, it's hard to evaluate whether or not the qualification are appropriate.

The second résumé states that the person is looking for a position in management. Immediately, the personnel director can call to mind a current opening plus the skills or criteria she uses to evaluate a good manager. When she reviews the résumé, she'll look for examples of organizational skills, communications skills, examples of leadership, and budgeting experience. In short, she'll have enough information to evaluate your minimum qualifications for the position.

Be careful not to make your objective either too general or too narrow. "Seeking a position which will utilize academic achievements and hands-on experience while providing for career development opportunities" could hardly help a job hunter's candidacy. As a personnel director, I would not have any idea what that career objective offered me as an employer, except someone who wanted to be promoted. Hardly a good first impression. On the other hand, "Seeking a management position in a hospital, with responsibility for programs, budget, and staff supervision" could also work against you by eliminating you from other openings you might be equally qualified for.

Some of you may have to be more general, especially if you are blitzing several companies. "An entry-level position in sales" may be as close as you can come. In any case, try to include:

- What you want to do (function).
- At what level (internship, entry level, trainee, middle management, executive).
- In what setting (financial institution, aerospace industry, consumer products, health care, nonprofit, government service, technology, engineering, etc.).

The rest of the résumé should now demonstrate the qualifications named in your Career Objective.

Experienced Administrator Has Done Everything
Skills, Experience, and Accomplishments

Start with your experience. Remember that experience, as it appears on your résumé, is anything you've done that allows you to confirm your ability to perform the functions of the job you are responding to. This includes actual paid full-time or part-time work, internships, volunteer work, and leadership positions in clubs and organizations, athletics, musical or dramatic competitions.

For instance, the skills acquired as an inventory clerk might well translate into the skills necessary for billing in a doctor's or lawyer's office. A first grade teacher might translate her experience into adult education or training and development in the corporate world. A bank loan officer probably has the marketing and analytical skills required of a credit officer. A flight attendant might package himself as a customer service representative for a manufacturing company because taking care of people and their complaints is part of both jobs.

"Don't just say, 'I was responsible for this and responsible for that,'" advises Richard Fuchs, president of Karli & Associates, a Dallas-based outplacement and career counseling firm. "They don't want to hear what you were responsible for. Companies want to hear about results, what you accomplished."

"Show how, within the scope of your current job, your work made a difference. However minor the results may seem, a prospective employer likes to know you're aware that work should produce results—a job is more than simply performing the tasks in a job description. Bottom-line results are especially important," advises career columnist Marilyn Moats Kennedy. Most companies give little or no consideration to résumés that do not clearly point to the person's impact on company productivity—increased sales, reduced costs, improved output—anything that reflects positively on the bottom line. What is it you may have to contribute that others may not? You need to communicate that what you offer will truly add value to the organization. Again I emphasize, be specific. Rather than stating "top-producing, inventive engineer," try listing a few of the patents you received. Instead of just "Purchased all office equipment," a more powerful statement might say, "Researched and evaluated office equipment vendors for best prices and quality; negotiated all prices and terms."

We looked at Ellie's experience and how that supported her Career Objective. We started by reviewing the candidate specifications to determine where her strengths lay. Her retail experience covered her management skills well. Now she needed to think about how to present herself to the broadcasting world as an on-air personality.

We began by determining what it takes to be a good radio personality. What kind of credentials and skills did Ellie already have that would convince someone that she could do this? She took a hard look at her volunteer work in college. This led her into disk jockeying at weddings and special occasions through a freelance service operated by a friend, an activity she continued to pursue throughout her professional life as a manager. After some thought, she listed three skills categories: radio, communications, and management.

In the first category, radio skills, she listed the tasks she had done at the university radio station during her four years there, including on-air interviewing, writing, research, reporting, and technical work. She was able to edit some of her shows as well as her work as a music disk jockey into a presentation CD of her on-air and live experience. She would indicate on the bottom of her résumé that she was sending along a CD of her work.

She next looked at how she could transfer the skills she had acquired at her management position to the radio world. As a manager, she had provided training and prepared reports for corporate meetings and conferences regarding her own department. This had sharpened her communications skills, her ability to get her point across in a clear and succinct manner in a way that was both enjoyable and informative. She felt this was important in presenting on-air information. She also believed it was necessary for a radio host to be able to fend off crises and remain calm when everything around her was falling apart.

"I remember one time in particular," she told me. "The entire fall line arrived just after several people were transferred out of my department. Before I had a chance to reorganize, the Chief Executive Officer blew in for his annual 'walk-through.'"

On the appointed day, she escorted the CEO through her department in a calm and professional manner, answering his questions and discussing future trends. He never suspected her whole department was in disarray at that exact moment. She summarized this as, "demonstrated ability to think and act under pressure."

She again drew on her retail experience to document her ability to meet deadlines. The third skill Ellie felt was important in determining on-air potential was leadership.

171

"You have to create a following of people who are interested in listening to you," she told me. "You have to attract people who want to hear what you have to say and value what your program offers them." So she looked to the leadership skills she developed in her management program. *

The major challenge in turning nonpaid experience into a full-time job is to build sufficient credentials to make the new job seem a natural outgrowth of your previous experience rather than a radical departure. The realities of life are, however, that employers, and especially personnel departments, take a dim view of anything but paid work. You must clearly prove the significance of unpaid experience and how it relates to the job.

By taking the time to categorize each of your experiences into responsibilities, skills, and accomplishments, you set up a primary database from which a variety of résumés can come. In the future, simply update your files, eliminating those items that are outdated or no longer pertinent and plugging in new information as necessary. This is equally true for chronological résumés.

This kind of preparation mentally catalogs all your qualifications for specific positions and helps prepare you for the interview. Although you won't include everything on your résumé, you'll have very specific examples to cite when the employer asks you to describe your ability to work under pressure, or to describe your management style. You'll be prepared for a multitude of questions because you are now aware of the breadth and depth of your experiences and how they relate to the job you want. Once you have all of this in your computer, you have created a very malleable database from which you can mix and match your entire array of information into a multitude of résumés.

Next, go back to your basic list. Determine where you meet or exceed the employer's requirements for the position. There are five specific areas you should explore:

- **Education and Training**
  List specific educational and training qualifications. Then develop a description of relevant experience that qualifies you to successfully meet these criteria.

- **Knowledge**
  Particularly look for the functional knowledge required by the position (marketing, sales, procurement, manufacturing, distribution, engineering, accounting, finance, personnel) to determine what specific qualifications are required.

- **Experience**
  Look at the range of the position (budgeting, strategic planning, number of functions to be managed, number of people to be managed). See what experience you have had in those areas.

- **Personal Characteristics**
  What personal characteristics are essential for good job performance in this position? Can you show you have these?

- **Proficiencies**
  What certificates or licenses do you have? What computer programs are you capable of working with?

A word of caution: Misrepresentation of job responsibilities has become perhaps the most substantial form of résumé embellishment, and employers are leery of such dramatic action verbs as *achieved, streamlined, managed, implemented.* Many of these have been so abused they have become clichés and raise a flag to interviewers. As you develop your résumé, be sure you can back up your claims with specific examples. Also beware of empty jargon such as "innovative, hands-on achiever" or "strong experience."

With this in mind, look at your skills. This is most often addressed by category in a functional-style résumé. This format is particularly useful for career changers, who want to move from one industry to another, or for someone who has held a series of nonrelated jobs. This works well in these instances because it showcases skill groupings, not where you acquired the skills.

Be specific about the kinds of expertise you want recognized by the person reviewing your résumé. If, for example, you want a job in the advertising field, look for skills that prove your ability to produce material that increases sales or attendance, or creates media attention, and highlight these. Look for selling skills. If you used these or similar skills in three or four jobs, organize them by category. For example: Communication Skills, Sales Skills, Public Relations Skills, Artistic & Creative Skills. Under each of these major headings, list your accomplishments that verify these skills. Don't mention the work site where you used them at this time, only the responsibilities and accomplishments. Focus on those things that are most important to the employer, those that the employer perceives to be important to the achievement of the organization's long-term strategic goals.

If your degree is recent enough, take a look at any of your coursework that directly reflects your technical training and specialization. For example, if you have listed that you desire a position in management with computer companies and your degree is in Computer Science, it would be important to list additional coursework you had that gave you the communication and people skills needed in management, such as psychology, financial accounting, or debate. Don't list them all; five is a good average number.

*Ellie listed drama, speech, and psychology courses to add extra texture to her communications degree. *

What Format Is Best?
Functional vs. Traditional vs. Electronic

Be forewarned, functional résumés make many personnel directors uncomfortable. It's harder for them to figure out what you did where. They feel this approach is too involved for a résumé and that this information is more appropriate for the interview. Others feel the format is used to hide something, such as a spotty record or limited work experience. To make this format effective, you must make it easy for the recruiter to understand.

Unless you have a really compelling reason, your best bet is still the traditional chronological format, a job-by-job explanation of your work experience. It is especially effective for those with a steady progression of ever more responsible positions. In many instances, the format alone will keep you in the applicant pool. Recruiters like it because it's faster to read and easier to assess.

If you go this route, list your pertinent work history in descending order by date. List under each employer the skills, experience, and accomplishments that will be most valuable to your new employer, using the same techniques as in the functional format.

Today, 85 percent of companies with more than 500 employees and all companies with 1,000 or more electronically scan résumés. There is good news and bad news in this. As they say, first the good news. Electronic résumés have a longer shelf-life, according to Jim Lemke, Manager, Employment and Human Resources Information Systems, UCLA. Once the résumé has been scanned, it remains in the system until specifically removed. The criteria for categorizing a résumé are much more specific and consistent, relying on key words and job relationships, which means your résumé has a higher probability of getting seen by the right person. Electronic systems also file résumés under all appropriate categories, so if you don't fit the job you applied for, you could be routed to something more suitable. Scanning systems are color and gender blind.

On the other hand, to be effective, the electronic résumé must be able to communicate intelligently with the scanner. Most work on some form of key word search. Be sure all your skills are listed unambiguously. Be very specific. List all of the programs you've ever worked with. List whatever tools you've used. These translate to skills. Use dates, the more recent the better.

Start with your most recent skills, as some scanning systems only read the first eighty. Career columnist Joyce Lain Kennedy suggests you start your résumé with a skills paragraph—a paragraph made up of nothing but skill words. You then put these words into context in the body of the résumé.

"Read by itself, the key word paragraph doesn't make sense, but it gets your attention," assures Lemke. Your choice of résumé format depends on what your previous experience has been and which will be the most effective sales piece for you. Some examples are given at the end of the chapter.

*As Ellie was obviously changing careers and a traditional résumé would not support that change, she believed she had nothing to lose by using the functional style. *

Whom You Worked for and How Long
Experience History

If you're using the functional format, you now list your experience so the potential employer will know where and for how long you used these skills. List only the positions that validate the skills section of your résumé; eliminate nonsignificant positions. This is a straightforward list, giving the organization's name, location (city and state only), position(s) you held, and length of stay if longer than one year. Listing length of stay by months and years in specific blocks of time is a good idea, especially if you have a consistent work history.

There are some exceptions. For example, if you worked for the same organization every summer during college, rather than listing 6/87–9/87, 6/88–9/88, and so on, it will be easier for the employer to grasp if you list length of employment as "four consecutive summers."

A ten-year history of your experience is usually sufficient.

*In Ellie's case, she listed both her paid and unpaid positions under "Experience History." *

Enhancing Your Image
Selecting the Nonessentials

Including professional affiliations, awards, and honors or hobbies and interests is totally up to you. They provide additional texture to your résumé, but they are not necessary ingredients. They aid in creating your desired image, but you may find that precious space could be put to better use in some of the more critical categories. If you decide to include one or all of these special sections, list only those that strengthen your résumé or create some insight about the kind of person you are in terms of the company's goals.

Professional affiliations are the most obvious for inclusion. If you belong to professional organizations that benefit the employer, then by all means include them. Awards and honors give some understanding of the things you choose to excel in and the areas that you have been recognized for by other people. These are especially valuable if they have meaning to the company.

Hobbies and interests provide the employer with some clue as to how you define the quality of your life outside the working environment. They provide a general understanding of your personality, and how that fits with the organization's personality and that of the specific job. Mention a hobby only if you have demonstrable accomplishments in a field of serious endeavor or if your avocation suggests qualities that relate directly to job performance. As one of the functions of the résumé is to create a certain amount of curiosity about who you are to trigger an interview, ask yourself: "Does this snapshot of me do this? What information shows me off best?"

Broadly educated people who can "piggy-back" their skills will find this section of the résumé most valuable. For instance, listing fluency in a foreign language or computer expertise can be invaluable. "International experience" doesn't necessarily have to come from paid professional experience. Many employers also give weight to overseas living or study experience. If the job requires a high degree of eye–hand motor coordination, patience, and concentration, you might mention leisure interests which also require these abilities (e.g., model airplane construction, crocheting, sewing) advises Jo Danna, author of *Winning the Job Interview Game: Tips for the High Tech Era*. Are you a person who enjoys competition and group activity such as participating in team sports? Are you quiet and reflective in your nonworking hours, choosing to spend your time reading and involved in individual activities? Are you civic minded and involved in your community through volunteer work? Other examples of activities which involve occupational interests and abilities might be:

- Computer club
- Sketching, painting
- Writing short stories, poems

177

- Repairing cars
- Theater group
- Toastmasters
- Physical Fitness/Cycling
- Rotary Club

It is important to list the professional licenses you have achieved or will need to do the work listed as your Career Objective. Many professions require board certification. If yours is one, make sure you list that information clearly on your résumé. If you don't, more often than not the assumption is that you do not have it, and this could eliminate you from the applicant pool.

Beyond Degrees
Education

Next, you'll want to list your education. As a matter of form, list your most advanced degree and/or your most recent degree first. For clarity's sake, employers want to know the name of the institution, the degree (bachelor of arts, master of science, etc.), major area of study, emphasis (if you had one in your major), and graduation date, if it is recent.

It is a matter of individual choice whether you list any other degrees or training you might have.

Do not omit your education because it is limited. Enlarge upon it where possible by listing company programs and home-study courses, for instance. This shows a desire for self-education readily understood by a sympathetic employer, who (like you) may not have had the opportunity for extensive formal education. The same employer will not be sympathetic to attempts at bluffing an education you do not have. The information you list in any section of your résumé should first and foremost be truthful and reflect your qualifications for the kind of work you have listed as your Career Objective.

You should also include professional development opportunities outside a collegiate environment, such as on-the-job training programs or workshops and conferences you have attended that continue to advance your skill base.

*Here's where Ellie listed her management training programs. *

Many career counselors believe employers assume references will be given when asked for, and therefore the ubiquitous sentence, "References provided upon request," is unnecessary. Your résumé is just the first step in the marketing portion of your career search process. An employer will contact your references as one of the last things he does before making you a job offer. It's inappropriate to give information at the beginning of the process that will not be necessary until much later. You might want to keep a list of your references available during the interview portion of your job search in case you are asked for them at that time.

Putting It All Together
Effective Editing

Now it's time for the hard part: editing. The key to a good résumé is brevity. Your résumé should consist of short, well-written, action statements, rather than complete sentences, that provide the employer with a well-rounded picture of your Professional Self, emphasizing the significant things that get your point across in a relatively brief space.

*Now that all the material from her Personal Assessment had been organized, it was time for Ellie to refine it. Rustling through the papers, she looked dismayed.
"But look at what you have to work with," I encouraged.
Ellie groaned. "You mean after writing down everything in the world, I need to leave most of it out?" *

Whichever format you choose, it should take no more than two pages, with many employers preferring a one-page version. Remember that most employers will skim through a résumé to see if you meet minimum qualifications first. Make sure they can find them easily. Long and detailed résumés are often not given the attention they deserve because of time constraints.

If you are doing this on your own, you might want to get a second opinion at this point. Have a career counselor or a friend read what you've done, and ask them what message they get from it. Does it present your Professional Self as you have defined it? Refinements are easy at this point.

When Ellie returned the next week, she proudly placed the two-page résumé on my desk.

"Here it is. It's done." I reviewed it and agreed. Ellie's résumé resulted in interviews with four small, out-of-state radio stations. All of the stations tried to push her into management, but she remained firm in her initial goal to be an on-air personality. She was finally offered a position at an easy-listening station in Reno, Nevada.

A year later, she was promoted to program director for the station and was in that position for close to another year before she began to apply to larger radio stations in more significant markets with higher pay scales.

The last time I heard from Ellie, she was a program director for a large radio station in the San Francisco area, where she hoped to settle permanently. She had also taken on the additional risk of starting her own business: a special-events disk jockeying service, employing several eager but inexperienced college students.

*She believes she will eventually move away from programming and back into supervision because she knows she's good at it, and it will become a logical step. For now, she's happy where she is, in a work environment she finds exciting and personally rewarding, and her salary now matches what she was making when she left her retail management position. *

The type of commitment you demonstrate in developing a well-thought-out résumé is a good indicator of how serious you are about making a career change. If you are willing to dig deep enough to separate the appropriate elements of your Professional Self from all of life's experiences and present these in terms the company recognizes and appreciates, you'll be able to create the kind of résumé that makes employers want to know you better. To do that, they'll have to invite you for an interview.

ELLIE FAIRCHILD
125 E. Oak Street
San Francisco, CA 94596
415-555-5151

CAREER OBJECTIVE
An entry-level position in radio as an <u>on-air personality</u> providing an opportunity to utilize proven communication and organizational skills.

SIGNIFICANT SKILLS
Radio/Technical Skills
Four years of experience as an undergraduate working at a campus radio station. Responsibilities provided an opportunity to conduct on-air interviews on a variety of topics of interest to the campus community, format musical sequences, program news breaks, and provide technical assistance in the overall production and operation of a twenty-four-hour station. Anchored a two-hour call-in program featuring comments from listening audience as well as music. Ratings remained consistently high during the duration of the program.

Communication Skills
Throughout professional career have been responsible for the preparation and presentation of departmental annual reports to Regional Manager. Effectively communicated budget and personnel needs of department to supervisors, resulting in increases in both areas. Performance appraisals over a three-year period consistently ranked communication skills as superior. Have demonstrated ability to think under pressure and put people at ease, while communicating detailed information in an educational as well as entertaining manner.

Management Skills
Successfully managed Handbag and Accessories Department for a national department store located in the Bay Area. Responsible for all aspects of personnel, budget, and sales

182

for a department with annual sales of $250,000. Was promoted to department manager after completion of sales promotion which increased sales by 15 percent over a two-month period. Demonstrated strong commitment to team approach and welcomed comments from staff regarding management style.

EXPERIENCE HISTORY
KCSB Radio Station, University of California, Santa Barbara, four years
Macy's Department Store, San Francisco, CA, three years
Traveling Melodies DeeJay Services, San Francisco, CA, two years

EDUCATION & TRAINING
University of California, Santa Barbara
Bachelor of Arts, Communication Studies, June 1996
Macy's Department Store Executive Training Program, San Francisco, CA (one-year program)

Significant Course Work:
Fundamentals of Acting
Voice Laboratory
Social Aspects of Behavior
Human Information Processing
Principles of Communication and Language
Public Speaking

AWARDS & HONORS
American Association of University Women, Undergraduate Scholarship Recipient, two consecutive years
Macy's Circle of Excellence Award, 1986
Girls' Clubs of America, Certificate of Appreciation for Outstanding Volunteer Service, 2003

HOBBIES & INTERESTS
Competitive running and cycling, coaching girls' tennis, and writing short stories

References and audition tape available upon request

Traditional Chronological Résumé Format

Alice Palmer

425 Meigs Road   Santa
Barbara, CA 93109
(805) XXX-7688

OBJECTIVE
To obtain an entry-level account executive position that utilizes my communication skills and creative abilities.

EXPERIENCE
Design Intern Santa Barbara *Independent*, March 1998 to present. Create and design visual presentation of print advertising in weekly entertainment newspaper. Demonstrate ability to work under pressure and meet deadlines while developing quick and precise paste-up, layout, and type-spec'ing skills. Assist with weekly production of editorial layout. Work closely with advertising client representatives in interpretation and execution of advertising concepts.

Marketing Assistant International Transducer Corporation, August 1996 to March 1998.
Exhibited strong verbal and written skills in customer service capacity. Accountability and organization required in maintaining quotation records for accurate sales projections. Served as foreign sales representatives' liaison. Responsible for distribution of product literature and compilation of customer and competitor information files. Organized and executed ITC's participation in undersea technology trade show. Position required flexible interpersonal skills to interact with multilevel positions.

Fundraiser Charitable Funding Group, July 1996 to August 1996. Raised $2,500 in one-month period from community members for construction of park facility. Sensitivity and tact were imperative to encourage donations for memorial site construction from families of Vietnam veterans. Adapted and composed caller script, which was adopted as official script.

Office Manager UCSB Student Government Office, January 1995 to June 1996.
Supervisory and leadership abilities highlighted in the management of a five-person clerical staff. Formulated and maintained $35,000 operating budget. Communication skills emphasized in meeting participation. Oriented new student officers to office policies/ procedures, and equipment operation. Promoted professional relationship between student officers and permanent career staff members.

Fundraiser UCSB Annual Fund Program, October 1994 to January 1995.
Negotiated over $10,500 in pledges from UCSB parents and alumni. Recognized as top caller with a cumulative 47 percent pledge rate and an average gift of $102. Wide knowledge of campus programs proved beneficial. Initiative and persistent attitude were necessary to meet target goals.

EDUCATION
B.A., Communication Studies, July 1998
University of California, Santa Barbara

Additional Coursework
Santa Barbara Community College
      Introduction to Advertising
      Introduction to Graphic Design
      Introduction to Pagemaker

ACTIVITIES
Associated Students Advertising & Publicity Board, September 1994 to June 1996
Fulfilled positions of Newsletter Editor, Treasurer, and Fundraising Organizer.

UCSB Advertising Club, 1993 to 1994
As a member, participated in development of award-winning campaign for collegiate competition.

REFERENCES
Available upon request

JOHN S. FRANKLIN, CPE
1321 Greeley Street
Sudbury, MA 01776
(508) 443-5555

OBJECTIVES: Corporate Management
A highly capable manager of facilities operations and maintenance, occupancy services, space planning, capital forecasting and justification, budgeting and control, workload planning, and directing support activities in both aerospace and commercial industries.

KEY WORDS:
Certified Plant Engineer, space planning, engineering, new construction, lease negotiation, maintenance, communications services, energy conservation, environmental programs, government interface, budget forecasting, capital panning, occupancy services, A&E contracts, standards development, budget preparation, personnel training, performance scheduling, administrative control, technical direction, management of CPFF, T&M, and FP contracts, workload panning, occupancy services, capital forecasting and justification, budgeting and control, CMMS, MS Office, and PM5.

CAREER HISTORY
Raytheon Company, Goleta, California
1980–1995
Manager, Plant Engineering and Facilities
> Responsible for managing the division's $300M investment in facilities, space and utilities, providing space planning, engineering, new construction, lease negotiation, modernization of exiting facilities (including clean rooms), maintenance and communications services for the research, development, engineering and manufacturing of electronic systems. Directed energy conservation, safety and environmental programs, including hazardous waste generation and disposal, providing the interface for federal,

state, and local agencies, $11M budget development and oversight.

Polaroid Corporation, Cambridge, Massachusetts
1967–1980
Manager, Engineering and Occupancy
> Provided management for the Cambridge properties including space planning and forecasting, leasehold evaluation, capital planning, and occupancy services. Supervised A&E contracts, development of standards, budget preparation, and personnel training for Corporate Facilities organization.

Sylvania Electronic Systems, Waltham, Massachusetts
1962–1967
Project Engineer
> Developed facilities criteria and space planning for construction of buildings, utilities, and site for radar/missile facilities. Included performance scheduling, change order, and design criteria. Provided administrative and technical direction to field installation teams.

GD/Astronautics, San Diego, California
1959–1962
Installation Support Supervisor
> Provided administrative control and technical direction of subcontractors for the activation of Atlas missile complexes. Included management of CPFF, T&M, and FP contracts for installation, maintenance, validation, and spares provisioning for facilities and Ground Support Equipment.

TWA, Kansas City, Missouri
1958–1959
Senior Facilities Engineer
> Prepared designs for commercial jet aircraft facilities nationwide.

General Motors Corporation, Kansas City, Missouri
   1955–1958
Facilities Engineer
   Prepared designs for automotive production facilities.

EDUCATION
   MS Engineering Management—Northwestern University
   BS Mechanical Engineering—GMI

9   Interviewing with Confidence
Creating a Job-Winning Image

"The person who gets the job offer is not always the most qualified, but rather the one best able to articulate his or her qualifications for the job."

As you are keenly aware, the interview is now-or-never time. You can't afford to blow it, so make sure you're good at it. This is your job. As you work at it, you'll get better. Recognize it for what it is—performance art. You don't have to enjoy it, but you do have to do it well.

Most people judge you by the way you value yourself. You must display poise and self-assurance; you must project the impression that you have the utmost confidence in your ability to do an outstanding job in this new position. If you don't come across as confident, how can you expect the employer to feel confident in hiring you? Act timidly, and people will think of you as timid.

*   * Madeline Aguirre now commands a comfortable corner office in a multistoried building in downtown Los Angeles, with a sign on the door stating "Director of Corporate Training." A far cry from the day four years earlier that a shy, retiring, thirty-two-year-old Hispanic woman sat across from me, looking for an accounting position. She appeared to shrink into her chair. When she was asked to talk about herself, the words came out one by one, as if physically forced. She squirmed in her seat when asked to describe her accomplishments. When I pressed her to be more expansive, she blushed and told me how her parents had always taught her "it wasn't nice" to be "boastful," to "brag" about one's accomplishments. More than that, she wasn't sure she had much to boast about.*
    But she was here with a purpose.
    "I've been asked to come in for an interview," she said, then hesitated. "Too many times I've come away from the interview with nothing. I know I lose it right there, and to people I know are no more qualified than I." Here a spark of rage took hold. Her dark eyes snapped while her fist clenched, ready to

pound out her frustration on the chair arm. Here was a determined lady. I asked for some background.

During her high school and college years, Madeline had helped out in the family business, a Mexican restaurant in the Greater Los Angeles area. As expected of a good daughter, she had done whatever was necessary. She waited tables; she ordered food, filled water glasses, and cooked. Later, she took over the bookkeeping, filled out the required government forms, and ordered food supplies.

While at college, where she earned her B.S. in accounting, most of her classmates took advantage of school-sponsored internship programs, but Madeline had no time left for these. During campus recruiting interviews, when the prestigious public accounting firms asked about her work experience, she simply hung her head shyly, much like she did before me now, and said she had none. This cost her dearly. Most of her interview feedback acknowledged she had the necessary technical skills and experience, but the jobs also required someone who would be aggressive in generating clients and assertive in her dealings with them. In this she failed. Her technical skills came wrapped in a timid, diffident demeanor. She didn't seem as if she could do the job.

Although recruiters often pointed this out to her, she didn't understand what they meant and could never put this criticism into a useful perspective. Unable to acknowledge her real problem, but armed with her accounting degree, she continued to apply for professional positions, but with no better luck. She finally settled for a bookkeeping job, a position that did not require, nor pay for, her knowledge of accounting, a sore disappointment after her years of preparation. She was underemployed and undervalued, and her future prospects were bleak. Madeline wondered if she did indeed have the skills necessary for a more responsible job. Otherwise, why had she not landed one?

The first job turned out to be as disappointing as the salary, and before long she moved on to another. She continued to accept a series of paraprofessional positions from employers who maintained that if she accepted these lower positions and did the professional work, when a position that she was qualified for in the professional ranks became available, they would consider her. She tried to be patient and optimistic.

Fate stepped in at this point and dealt her another hard blow. Her mother became seriously ill, forcing her to leave her job, come back home, and help in the family restaurant again.

I looked at her résumé. I understood why employers saw her as a professional risk. Besides the interruption to help out in the family crisis, she had held none of her jobs for any sustained period of time, and I asked her why.

"I've never been given what I was promised. Sure, I've gotten good evaluations, but I've never been promoted. They were all the same, and all the work so boring. I left each job hoping the next one would be better." Her eyes began snapping again. "When it happened this last time, I knew I had to do something." This time, the first came down solidly on the chair.

"First, my new supervisor was hired at twice my salary. Then she couldn't do the job, and when they found out, I was asked to train her! But that's not the half of it. When they finally fired her because of incompetence, the department head asked me to fill in until a qualified person could be found. I told him I wanted to be considered for the position and gave him my résumé. He told me it was unusual for the organization to move someone from the support ranks to the professional ranks. It just was not done, and I would need a lot more experience. When I pointed out I had a bachelor's degree in accounting, he told me that I hadn't used my accounting since graduation and was too rusty for the job. My degree was no longer an asset, and my performance on the job counted for nothing. I quit that very day."

She went back to the restaurant business as an interim step while she continued her search for work in her chosen field.

She sent out résumés in response to several ads for accountants, and one of the companies finally asked her to come in for an interview. She passed the ad across my desk.

"I know I can do this job, but too many times, after the interview, I never hear from them again. I'm tired of that. Can you help me?" *

According to a study by Northwestern University of 405 top employers, the number-one reason for an applicant not getting the job is poor personality and manner; followed by lack of poise, poor presentation of self, lack of confidence, and a timid, hesitant approach.

Applying for a job often becomes a matter of persuading yourself that you're not stepping out of your league, that you're not misrepresenting yourself, that you're not faking it. Sometimes, it feels like an act, but once you present yourself confidently, people accept you as a self-assured person, and because people treat you as a confident, valuable person, a new Professional Self emerges. You become that new self.

The one central question in all interviews that often remains unspoken is, "Why should I hire you?" If you think of the interviewer as having this central objective in mind rather than simply scrutinizing your or picking you apart, you will interview more comfortably and effectively. Just keep "Why should *I* be hired?" in mind, and design every one of your responses so that it gives the employer another reason for choosing you. One common reason for nervousness going into a job interview is fear you won't get an offer. Just tell yourself that if you don't get an offer, you're no worse off than before.

I call the interview the "two head test." You can assume the organization sees you as at least minimally qualified since you made it to the interview stage. Now they want to see what you look like and how you operate in a stressful situation. This is the time when they evaluate your personality style and your personal strengths and abilities. That's why it's so important to be well prepared.

Remember that although the interviewer controls the flow of the interview, you control its content.

You are responsible for making the interview interesting and informative. Keep in mind the interview is *your* opportunity let the employer know you understand that although others are also qualified, you are the *best* candidate because you bring assets to the organization that are uniquely your own. By hiring you, the organization will benefit from all the other skills and abilities you have mastered and gathered during your lifetime. Focus on those things the employer perceives to be important to the achievement of the organization's long-term strategic goals. The more the interviewer perceives you as possessing these capabilities, the greater your chances of getting an offer.

*　We put the ad Madeline had answered in front of us and broke it down into individual skills. We culled from her experience and skills those that fit the specifics of the job in front of us, much as Pat did in Chapter 3.*

Next, we addressed her work history. She retreated again. "My present employment is at the restaurant," she reminded me.

I asked her to tell me exactly what she did there.

Slowly, she began to recount her current responsibilities. "I hire the staff. I train the new employees," she began. It turned out she also ordered all food and supplies, and was, in fact, the financial officer and chief accountant for the organization. Her books were regularly audited, and each time she received compliments on their completeness and accuracy. She had obviously put her accounting background to good use.

Next, we delved into her volunteer work, the clubs and organizations she belonged to, her travel experiences.

"Let's see. After the Guatemalan earthquake, I helped organize food supplies to be sent to refugees. As a matter of fact, I was between jobs just then, so I went there and stayed for six months training other volunteers. My Spanish came in handy."

*After further review, we added language and writing to her skills list. *

You must describe your skills in concise, unambiguous terms; back up your claims by referring to actual experiences in your life; and make a clear connection between your skills and the needs of the employer.

There are two parts to every interview:

- You must convince the company that you have the necessary experience and skills to do the job.

- You must persuade the interviewer that your unique life experiences will benefit the organization.

The extras you provide will make a difference when the employer decides who is the "most" qualified. The employer sees this as the candidate who will make the biggest contribution above and beyond the specifics of the job.

Creating the Sizzle
Establishing Your Experience and Skills

Your first step is to identify what you gained from your experiences and how that applies to the position at hand. You need to think carefully about the conceptual similarities that exist between this job and the other jobs you've held. That way, when you hear an objection about the differences between your experience and the company's requirements, you can counter with the similarities. Then give examples to support this. In sales, this is called "overcoming objections."

Look for ways to "piggy-back" your skills. People who can do this will not only be the most marketable, but also the most promotable and the highest paid, according to Maxine Wineapple, President of New Options Program, a career counseling service. As an example, a degree in computer science will open many doors, but a fluency in Japanese increases the computer scientist's opportunities dramatically. Add to that management expertise, and the Japanese-speaking computer scientist is virtually assured entree into a fast-track career, she points out.

＊ Madeline made notes, organized around the specific skills and experiences required for this particular job. She looked for where she had developed these skills and experiences and how she used them in particular tasks. She needed to learn not to trivialize her assets, but to imagine contexts where they could be

194

useful. The quieter you keep about your strengths, the more easily they tend to fade into the woodwork and become invisible even to yourself, as Madeline had found. *

Selling What You Will Do for the Company
Adding Value to Your Candidacy

The next step is selling the company on what you can do for it. Begin by studying the company itself.

The shortest interview I ever witnessed was at a west coast university.

Motorola was interviewing graduating seniors for entry-level positions. Adam, a very qualified student, entered the interview room only to emerge a scant two minutes later, ashen faced, astonished, and dismayed. Once he recovered from the shock, he told me the first thing the interviewer asked was what he knew about the company. Adam began by saying what great televisions Motorola made and how his family had purchased them for years.

The interviewer asked Adam if he had read the information the company had sent to the campus recruiting office on this particular Motorola division. Surprised, he responded he had not, but he planned to do so as soon as the interview was over.

The interviewer stood up and shook his hand, said the interview was over, and showed him the door. If Adam had done his homework, he would have learned this particular division of Motorola was the Satellite Division and had no connection at all with TV's.

Employers expect you to know what you are interviewing for, what the organization's products and services are, whom they serve, their location, and other pertinent information regarding the organization and to incorporate that information into your answers during the interview.

* I outlined the steps in Chapter 6 on research, and Madeline went to work.

She returned the next week, notes in hand. She had learned from the company's annual report that it had recently purchased a business that provided packaged meals for four major business cafeterias in the area. She was excited to see how she could relate her accounting degree, her restaurant experience, and her other volunteer experience to the organization. *

The interviewer may try to find out how well you have prepared by asking you to comment on your own career path within the company. Think about this carefully in terms of the goals of the organization so that the interviewer will know your career goals are realistic within the organization's structure and that this position is a logical step.

Even if not asked directly, having this information at hand enhances your own comfort level. You can also use this information effectively at the end of the interview, when asked, "Do you have any questions?"

Interviewers are always trying to fill specific positions. There will be certain characteristics they will be looking for, including your past performance, as they believe this to be the single best predictor of success in the future. Prepare examples of times you've used a variety of skills in situations that are similar to the ones listed in the job description. When the interviewer asks, "How would you handle…" or "Give me an example of…" he or she is looking for clues to how you process information, develop solutions, or tackle problems. Don't concern yourself so much with whether the answer is right, but rather focus on the process by which you arrived at the solution, and be prepared to provide details about that process. Back up your statements with examples, illustrations, descriptions, statistics, comparisons, or testimonials. This helps clarify your comments, helps substantiate them, helps the listener remember them, and adds interest to your presentation. Always, always affirm the positive and sound confident.

"No boss will pay you to prove that you can do something you haven't already done. First, he wants to see you solve the problems he hired you to solve," says New York management consultant Martin Yate, author of *Knock 'em Dead: With Great Answers to Interview Questions*. The more closely your research determines what these particulars are and how you have used them, the more qualified you appear.

On the other hand, don't worry if you haven't done everything. As a general guideline, I like to use what I call the 50–30–20 rule. You should be 100 percent proficient at 50 percent of the job. You should be able to become proficient in 30 percent of the job in three to six months, given proper training and orientation. And 20 percent of the job should be totally new to you.

If you are 100 percent qualified the day you walk into the job, you are also overqualified and underpaid from that day on. Having half the job in the bag is your assurance to employers that they are getting their money's worth. The next 30 percent is the employer's commitment to you as a working professional. The last 20 percent is your commitment to yourself to continue your own growth and increase your skills bank with each new position.

The 50–30–20 rule is part of the concept of Positioning I wrote about in Chapter 1. When you have mastered a job at 100 percent, then it is time for you to reevaluate your employment situation. Remember, you work to provide a livelihood for yourself and those who depend on you. If you are doing a job at 100 percent, you are now overqualified and underpaid.

You are faced with some choices. Am I happy with my current situation and salary? What more do I want to learn in this position? Are there other positions within the organization I would like to move into? What other options are available to me outside the organization? These questions and more should be going through your head as you evaluate your next career decision.

This is career planning and career consumerism at it best. When you intuitively begin to evaluate your career as you would any other business equation, you are in the Career Consumer Hall of Fame! This is the time when, in the course of your career development, you realize you have power over your career. You realize that your ability to provide an income for yourself and your family is completely in your hands.

This is not a pipe dream; this is a realization of your own worth in the employment milieu. Don't think for a minute the rest of the world is going to realize what a stellar person you are, but the knowledge of your own self-worth is everything. It will help you move those mountains that lie ahead.

I asked Madeline to think back on the work we had done and to determine how she might truly add value to this employer's organization.

*Madeline's responsibility during the interview was to demonstrate both verbally and by her presence this uniqueness and individuality. Professional recruiters often complain that candidates are not verbal enough and do not give concrete examples of their experience and how it pertains to their professional potential. This had certainly been true of Madeline. ***

During a behavior-based interview, it is important that you give specific examples of experiences in your life that have provided you an opportunity to use the same skills necessary on the job.

Don't be reluctant to talk about yourself and your accomplishments. Remember, the interviewer wants to know more about you, especially your potential value to the organization. The more information you can communicate, the stronger your position will be.

As you prepare for your interview, testing your strategy can significantly improve your chances of success. Now is a good time to arrange for a mock interview with a career counselor, or at least a good, objective friend. It will help to clarify your presentation both in style and content. It's hard for you to see the big picture when you're standing in the frame.

Stacking the Deck in Your Favor
Selling Yourself

It all comes down to the forty-five minutes you spend face to face with the interviewer. In study after study, employers say the job interview is the single most important activity in determining whom they hire.

John L. Lafevre, in his book *A Peek Inside the Recruiter's Briefcase*, describes interviewers as "merely professional gamblers who have been provided a thirty-minute tip-sheet analysis to help them decide on which candidate to place the bet." In fact, most decisions are made on visceral reactions to interviewees by the person making the decision. And quite possibly the decision will be made by the time you sit down. Your basic objective is to spark a positive feeling from the time you step into the office.

The interviewer wants to confirm this spot decision. He wants to know who you are as a person, as an individual with a certain amount of uniqueness. This is your chance to show your stuff, the place where your motivations and the employer's needs come together.

That's not always easy. People from other cultural backgrounds often have their confidence eroded by negotiating in a different society. One of the factors often facing first-generation college graduates, many of whom are minorities and women, is that no one has gone before them who can tell them what it's like.

"People may know very little about the communication system of African Americans or Asians," according to management consultant, Onolee Zwicke, who points out that some cultures are traditionally demonstrative, whereas others are more restrained. If their culture has socialized them to be nonassertive by Western standards, they may have learned to be modest, self-effacing, reserved, quiet, or dependent on others. Self-deprecation becomes a ritual way of getting information out without appearing to boast, but interviewers often take this modest demeanor as a genuine lack of self-confidence. For these reasons, women and people of color may find it especially challenging to be forthright about their own strengths and achievements. But you must get straight with yourself that you have something to offer, and you must be willing to say it to anyone who needs to hear it.

* No one in Madeline's family had interviewed for a professional situation. She had no idea of the kind of information that needed to be shared and did not know how to prepare. As a result, she walked into an interview feeling terrorized by her

*ignorance and too intimidated to express herself well. Simply put, good interviewing is good salesmanship. The people she lost to were just better able to sell themselves. ***

It is not outrageous to say in an interview, "I know I can do the job you want done, and I have plenty of examples to back up what I'm saying." That isn't cocky. It's an honest expression of your belief in yourself, regardless of what the other candidates may have in their backgrounds.

Interviewing for a job is a truly American practice and until recently, one dominated by white males. Other countries' employment traditions appear strange to Americans, who are often unsuccessful in their initial interviews abroad because they rely on how it's done here at home.

What we're talking about are the tools for survival in the American marketplace. One of the basic skills for success is interviewing well. It is as basic as learning to write. By injecting your own personality into the interview, you let the employer know that you value yourself as a person, you like who you are, and believe that, in addition to your professional qualifications, you have many other qualities to offer the employer who is lucky enough to hire you.

* Body language was especially important in Madeline's case. She was quite small in stature, and when she compressed herself into her chair, she appeared frail and birdlike. We began with a difficult discussion on how she could project the necessary confidence. Being a Hispanic woman myself, I pointed out how we both use our hands when we speak, and how these gestures are a part of our communication style. Madeline agreed, and yet, before me now, she sat quietly, her hands under careful control. She felt the natural effervescence she displayed in social situations was inappropriate in the workplace. "It's appropriate if used in a way that exhibits your comfort level with yourself," I told her.

I assured Madeline that it was not necessary to jeopardize her cultural background or to assume she had to adopt this style in other areas of her life.

Next, I asked her to describe herself, what she brought to the table. Here, she smacked solidly into a mental wall, finding nothing to say beyond her résumé, again a common reaction. *

To help my clients understand their own personal skills and abilities, I begin by asking how three of their best friends would describe them. Describing themselves in the third person feels more comfortable at first, and with practice they are soon able to articulate their distinctiveness and not feel uncomfortable or boastful.

Here are some questions I ask to get them started:

- Are you the person in your group who always balances the check after dinner, determining how much everybody pays? (eye for detail, good with money)
- Are you the one who can organize a party on a moment's notice, complete with hats and horns? (a doer, someone who gets things done, spontaneous)
- Do people come to you as a sounding board when they need some clarity on a problem they are having? (trustworthy, good problem solver, creative)
- Are you artistic?
- Just what is it that your friends value in you? What skills do these suggest?

For instance, the compulsive person who does everything in the same order according to schedule is also the person who keeps perfect and orderly records of all calls, correspondence, and visitors. The confrontational person who can't help being very direct with people, is the same person who can approach customers who are behind in their payments. Note if you have a well-developed sense of humor, are very organized, put people at ease, or are creative, and begin to develop a plan for incorporating those strengths into your professional profile.

It also helps to start letting your friends know when you've done something that makes you proud. Tell them when you've had a success. Call your family when you've accomplished something that makes you proud. Tell your boss or co-workers about projects you've completed or problems you've solved. You may feel

201

uncomfortable talking about yourself at first, but keep in mind that, as with anything else, you will improve with practice. It gets easier as your confidence builds, and it is confidence that separates the successful from the also-rans.

> *Self-confidence is based on an honest, unabashed comfort with your skills and abilities.*

Self-confidence manifests itself in your behavior. Even if this is difficult, if you make the interviewer think you believe in yourself, you'll be on the right track.

If a lack of confidence is persistent and you cannot seem to rid yourself of these feelings no matter what you do, you might want to explore where your feelings come from with a counselor. General feelings of low self-esteem will continually hamper your job search if you leave them unattended.

Inevitably, during the course of the interviewing process you will see other candidates who will impress you and you'll imagine you don't have a chance. Don't assume yourself into a position where style rather than essence intimidates you.

> *The person who gets the job offer is not necessarily the most qualified, but rather the one best able to articulate his or her qualifications. Your job is to make sure that person is you.*

Putting Yourself in Control
Basic Preparation

Break down everything you've learned about yourself and about the company so far into the five major areas the interviewer will want to get at:

- Educational history
- Work and experience
- Personal skills and attributes

- Career and professional goals
- Knowledge of the organization

File all your information under these five categories. When asked a question, you'll be able to determine quickly which of the five mental files to access.

An important goal of any job interview should be to obtain useful information to determine whether the job is right for you. Is this a "good fit?" Is the "corporate culture" one you understand and can function with? Success in the interview may mean learning that the position is not for you. If you see your goal as gathering information, you're more likely to perform better. This is not a win-lose game, but an exchange of useful information between you both. Level the playing field by giving the employer the information he or she needs to hear from you in an orderly, confident, and interesting manner. Your use of examples and anecdotal information will showcase your skills and qualifications within the framework of a story.

To make the interview a relaxed, mutual exchange of information, you must have a flexible agenda of the points you want to raise. This helps you maintain control. That control, whether real or psychological, can go a long way in maintaining your composure during the initial interview and in subsequent meetings. Now is the time to query the interviewer on how he or she views the position and the tasks he or she wants accomplished. Get this information as early in the interview as possible so that you can tailor your experience and skills to the needs he or she reveals.

You must be comfortable in the interview setting in order to make the best impression. One good way to do this is to know in advance how you'll respond to a variety of questions an interviewer might pose. There are a number of commonly asked questions you can anticipate. For instance, interviewers may probe your decision-making approaches with questions such as:

"I'm curious to know what you would do if…"

"What were your three most important responsibilities in that job?"

"What special skills or knowledge did you need to perform these duties?"

Other common questions, especially if your job experience is limited, are:

"What do you see as your best quality? Your worst?"

"What was your most difficult class in college, and what did you learn from it?"

"Which one of your skills do you think you will use most in this position, and why?"

(A list of fifty most commonly asked questions will be found at the end of this chapter.)

These questions generally reduce to one of three varieties:

Why us? Why have you chosen to apply here? What interests you about our organization?

Why you? Why should we be especially interested in you over others?

Why now? What makes this the right time for you and us?

Although I don't suggest memorizing a series of answers that will sound stiff and unnatural, I do encourage you to develop an outline of areas you would like to cover in your interview and come with ideas on how to respond if asked these questions. Practice your responses so that you present your qualifications and individuality well. Do this enough times before the interview so that they sound comfortable coming out of your mouth, like you are talking about someone you know very well, not someone you've just met. Your interviewing style showcases the information from the personal database you presented on your résumé and any other information you feel is appropriate to the position.

I must emphasize how important it is to practice your answers out loud. One method I find to be exceptionally helpful is to use a tape recorder and then play the answers back for review. How do you sound? Are there a lot of pauses, "ahems," and "you knows" in your answers? Ask yourself, if you were in the interviewer's position, would you hire the person on the tape? Repeating your answers three or four times, or having someone else critique them, will generate a certain amount of comfort on your part and improve the quality of your responses.

Madeline returned the next week looking composed and confident.

"I can't tell you how uncomfortable it was to practice out loud," she confessed after her first attempt with the tape recorder. She stumbled on nearly all of the sample questions.

"My mind either drew an immediate blank, or I rambled on and on. Sometimes I just spouted nonsense." But she stuck to it, thought each question through, and tried again. Her goal was to paint a verbal picture of herself as someone capable of performing the functions and responsibilities cited in the job description. She confronted herself in front of a mirror, and when she was confident with that, she gave the list of questions to her roommate and asked her to pick ten random questions. When she was comfortable with this, she went back to the mirror for more polish with those she felt were the most important. *

As I said before, examples are important; they demonstrate that you have prepared and given the interview some thought before hand. Go through a series of practice interviews. If you are not working with a career counselor, enlist the help of a neighbor, a friend, or a significant other—someone who can offer an unbiased opinion of your interview style.

Identify three anecdotes or examples that illustrate your qualifications for the job, stories that tell of your uncovering specific issues while conducting research for the interview, reviews of past experiences, sincere expressions of motivations, or interesting examples of your most significant accomplishments. Practice your answers while you are dressing in the morning. Look at yourself in the mirror. Do you look relaxed? Can you meet your own gaze in the mirror? Will you be able to look directly at the interviewer? With practice, these things become naturally incorporated into your repertoire of responses.

The final preparation is for the last two commonly asked questions: "Is there anything you'd like to add?" and "Do you have any questions to ask me?"

In response to "Is there anything you'd like to add?" always restate your interest in the position and underscore your qualifications or skills. If the interviewer failed to ask questions that allowed you to talk about your chief qualities, bring them up now. Be sure to reread your résumé before the interview to remind yourself of the key points you want to get across.

Your response to "Do you have any questions to ask me?" depends on what has previously occurred. Ideally, you will have already familiarized yourself with the occupational field in general and the interviewing organization in particular. Then, you will have framed some questions that are of critical importance to you in line with your career goals. Be sure you cover them. Some questions you might want to consider are:

"What created the job opening?"
"How will my performance be measured?
"What are you looking for in a candidate for this position?

Confidence problems can be dealt with and improved, as Madeline demonstrated as we practiced together. She soon found her nervousness and discomfort level easing. She began to list what made her different: her bilingual abilities, the tact and diplomacy she had learned from years in the restaurant business, and the ability to stick to a task until completion.

*"I'll never remember it all," Madeline lamented, shuffling through her research. "I know I'll forget something important." ***

If you have to, put your final questions on small file cards. Look them over to see that everything has been addressed. By developing questions prior to the interview, you demonstrate concern about the position as well as preparation for the interview. Most interviewers will view you in a positive manner if you do this. Questions about the business side of the firm are also valuable because they mark you as a serious, ambitious candidate with a definite future. If your interviewer gives embarrassed or evasive answers to any of the questions, you can be sure there is something to be embarrassed or evasive about.

If the interviewer was very thorough, the only question might be, "When can I expect to hear from you?" or "When will you be making your hiring decision?"

If you are asked back for a second interview, you'll prepare essentially the same as for the first. Most likely, this will be with a different person, so all your initial information will be new.

You might want to review your first interview. Here is the perfect opportunity to use 20/20 hindsight. What could you have done better? What did you forget that you wished you had said? What good examples have you just remembered? What were the really strong points you want to reemphasize?

Whether it is a screening interview or a selection interview, you should know who is to make the next move, and what that move is to be. Do you need to furnish more information—a transcript, a completed application, references, an example of your work? Will the employer get in touch with you, or you with him or her? Approximately when?

In addition, if the interview was for selection purposes, you should know the duties of the position, the supervisory structure, the employer's expectations of you, the working environment, the reason for the opening (newly created, resignation, promotion, reorganization, or the company's expansion into a new market), the salary range, and benefits. This is usually the time references are brought up.

My Biggest Fans
References

Choose people who can speak to your qualifications for this particular job. Make sure you've talked to them about the kind of employment you're looking for and why you think they can speak to your qualifications. Give them a copy of your résumé and any pertinent information that will make their recommendation stronger and more personal.

Professional recruiters are always able to spot references that have had only minimal contact with the perspective employee and conversely are able to spot those who know them well. Follow up with your references regarding the status of your job search, and make sure to send the appropriate thank-you notes once you've gotten the job. This kind of follow-up ensures a good, professional memory for your references and enhances your changes of using them in the future.

The Time, the Place, and Looking the Part
Nitty-Gritty Common Sense

It is important that you be on time. Punctuality is essential. If you are scheduled for an on-site interview, it is a good idea to call ahead and ask where you should park, what office you need to report to, and how long the interview will be. This is particularly important if you are interviewing in another city or with a large organization where you might have to pass through a security clearance.

If you know in advance what to expect, there should be no surprises that may cause you to be late or miss the interview entirely, such as one applicant who missed a tricky freeway exit. She was fifteen minutes late for the meeting. The interviewer informed her he had allowed her thirty minutes to make her case, and she had already used up half of that. I know of another instance in which the company name was not on the building.

Appropriate dress is very important. If you want to be taken seriously as a professional, you must look like a professional. For both men and women, a suit is a must. More often than not, you will dress more formally for the interview than you will for the job. This was true for one man who was applying for a position where he would wear coveralls. He impressed the employer when he appeared for the interview in his only suit, and he got the job.

*Madeline did not trust her own fashion sense. Her wardrobe was heavily weighted toward the casual and comfortable. I suggested she talk to a salesperson in a department store or a dress shop, giving her an idea of the kind of organization she was interviewing with, the kind of position she was seeking, and the amount of money she wanted to spend. *

If you believe your own wardrobe is inadequate, visit a good clothing store and tell them what you're looking for. Make your request comprehensive. Say, for instance, "This is the kind of job I'm interviewing for, and I need everything for $250: shoes, stockings, accessories, everything." The salesperson should either throw you right out of her store or be able to put together two or three outfits for you to select from, but plan on at least two trips to complete the job. For the truly adventurous and budget conscious, I would recommend calling local thrift shops and secondhand stores to find out if they have a section of suits and professional clothes. You would be astonished at what you will sometimes find. I took several students out on a shopping expedition right after the store had done a clothes drive in one of the most exclusive parts of town. Not only were brand and designer labels available, there were couture outfits made specifically for whoever had donated to the thrift store. For $100 each, my students walked out with a Versace jacket dress perfect for an interview with a real estate eveloper in San Francisco and a Stella McCartney pinstriped skirt suit that would fit right in at a Universal Studios interview later that month. Hermes bags and Manolo pumps finished off their ensembles.

Another tip, if you are an older person. "Look as young as possible," according to Gary Kravetz, owner of National Career Choices, an executive and technical employee recruiting company. If you have gray hair and a few wrinkles, at least look young at heart, and act that way, he advises. Don't overdo it, but don't come across as old and tired. "Enthusiasm helps," he says, and a brand new computer science degree is worth touting.

Mastering the art of interviewing is essential to your successful job search. If you can relax and enjoy it, so much the better. But first and foremost, you must practice and become good at it!

All her preparation did not prevent Madeline's palms from sweating, but it did give her the presence of mind during the interview to evaluate whether this organization met her employment needs rather than worrying abut what she was going to be asked next. By the end of the hour, to her surprise, she was enjoying herself. As she left, she was told a final decision would be made within the week, and she would be contacted. She left with confidence. It was justified. A week later, the interviewer called Madeline and offered her the position. But that is not the end of the story.

As we reviewed the job offer, Madeline paused.

"Ever since the interview, I've been thinking about their new food service division. If it's going to be successful, the employees are going to need a lot of training, and right away. I wonder if they've thought about that?"

"Maybe not. Why not bring it up in your letter of acceptance?"

She did and was asked to come in for another interview, this time specifically to discuss her ideas about a training program. The company was impressed. She was asked to help develop the new program and was appointed its first director. Madeline is now proud of herself, and proud of her job; she is a valued employee and a great source of pride to her family.

Madeline is a classic example of a career seeker who starts a search aiming toward one goal and midstream adjusts that original goal to accommodate the new insights generated while working through The Professional Self Model. *

Fifty Questions Frequently Asked at Interviews

1. What can I do for you?
2. Why did you contact me?
3. Why do you want to work for us?
4. What can you do for us?
5. How do you think you would fit into our operations?
6. What do you know about our company?
7. Tell me about yourself.
8. Have you any experience in supervision?
9. How did you get into your field?
10. Does your employer know that you are planning to leave?
11. Why do you want to leave your present position? Why did you leave your last job?
12. Have you ever been fired from a job? Why or why not?
13. Why have you been unemployed for so long?
14. Why have you held so many jobs?
15. What was your salary in your previous position?
16. What are your current salary requirements?
17. Why do you want to change fields now?
18. Aren't you overqualified for this position?
19. What are your general feelings about _____ *?
    (*Women in business, unions, sales production, personnel, management, politics?)
20. Do you have any objections to a psychological interview and tests?
21. What is your philosophy of life?
22. Have you ever thought about going into business for yourself?
23. What goals did you set for yourself this year, and how well have you done toward accomplishing them? Why?
24. What are your professional five-year goals?
25. What are your personal five-year goals?
26. How was the (last employer) company as a place to work?
27. What did you like best about your old job? What did you like least?
28. What would you rather have done more of in your last position? Why?

29. If you could have made one suggestion to management in your last job, what would it have been? Why?
30. What do you consider your worst/best attribute?
31. What was the hardest thing you've ever done? Why?
32. What do you regard as your strongest qualification for this job?
33. What do you think is likely to make the difference between success and failure in this position?
34. What do you feel has been your greatest accomplishment in life? Why?
35. What have been your three most noteworthy accomplishments in the past year? Why?
36. What has been your greatest disappointment? Why?
37. What are three of your strongest points? What are three of your weakest points?
38. What have you done in the past year to improve yourself?
39. What factors in your past have contributed most to your development?
40. What factors would you say may have been handicaps in preventing you from moving ahead more quickly?
41. Would you mind moving away from this area?
42. How would you solve this problem of ours?
43. What qualities do you think this company should look for in an applicant for this position?
44. As an employee, what can management do to assist you in functioning effectively?
45. If you are hired, how do you visualize your future with this company?
46. Do you have any other questions?
47. What are your favorite charities, and how do you contribute to them?
48. What interests you most about this position?
49. How would you describe your work experience so far?
50. Why should we hire you?

Sixteen Attributes Sought by Employers

The National Association of Colleges and Employers has listed sixteen attributes employers are looking for. No one interviewer will cover all of these attributes, but they are good indicators of what the selection process is all about and how you can plan for the interview.

Ability to Communicate. Do you have the ability to organize your thoughts effectively? Can you express them clearly when speaking or writing? Are you persuasive?

Intelligence. Do you have the ability to understand and conduct the job assignment? Can you learn the specific operations? Will you be able to contribute original ideas or actions?

Self-Confidence. Are you mature? Can you deal positively and effectively with situations and people? Are you secure about your abilities?

Willingness to Accept Responsibility. Can you recognize what needs to be done and set about doing it?

Initiative. Do you have the ability to identify the purpose for work and to take action? Can you set goals and objectives?

Leadership. Can you guide and direct others to obtain the recognized objectives?

Energy Level. Do you demonstrate a forcefulness and capacity to move things ahead? Can you maintain your work effort over a period of time and at a sustained rate?

Imagination. Can you conceptualize new situations and form solutions to them? Do you find new answers in standard approaches to problems?

Flexibility. Are you capable of changing? Are you receptive to new ways of doing things, new locations, new people?

Interpersonal Skills. Can you bring out the best in people to help them become effective, enthusiastic members of the work team?

Self-Knowledge. Can you realistically assess your capabilities? Can you identify your strengths and weaknesses? Do you know what skills you bring to a job?

Ability to Handle Conflict. Can you contend with stressful situations and antagonism? Can you resolve conflicts with others without personal attacks? Do you have a practiced approach to conflict resolution?

Competitiveness. Do you have a willingness to be measured by your performance in relation to that of others?

Goal Achievement. Can you identify goals and work toward them? Are you challenged by goals?

Skills. Do you have the right combination of education (or training) and skills required for the job you are seeking? Are your skills up to date?

Direction. Have you determined your personal values and needs? Have you reflected on your interests? Have you determined what type of job or occupation will satisfy these things, plus your skills and goals?

*

"There's an old story about three workers breaking up rocks. When the first was asked what he was doing, he replied, 'Making little ones out of big ones;' the second said, 'Making a living;' and the third, 'Building a cathedral.'" — John Julian Ryan

*

"If people feel they have control over their destinies they will persist at tasks." — Tom Peters and Robert Waterman

*

"Job-hunting is stressful, time-consuming, labor-intensive, and low-paying." Scott Badler

*

"I think I'll work all my life. When you're having fun, why stop having fun?" — Helen Thomas

*

10   Negotiating
The Slow Dance of Job Search

"Knowing what to go for, when to go for it, when to back off."

An initial offer of the minimum package is not unusual. Whether or not you can move beyond this depends on your skills and experience and the employer's flexibility. Asking for what you want is probably the most difficult step in the job search process, whether you're a secretary or a division manager or the CEO. Whatever your level, the steps and principles are the same.

- Determine what's feasible.
- Identify what you want.
- Discuss your requirements.
- Plan your strategy.
- Present your plan.
- Identify your allies.
- Reintroduce the remaining topics.
- Evaluate the offer.
- Follow up.
- Reinforce the negotiated topics.

A prestigious San Francisco medical group had offered Dr. Robert Moffett a position as a staff surgeon, and he knew he wanted the job. He had grown up in the Bay Area and wanted to return. The facility was close to the University of California, San Francisco Medical School and the University of California, Berkeley—both first-class research institutions—and he wanted to stay on the cutting edge of his field.

"One of the reasons I chose surgery," he confided, "is because nine times out of ten the patients are unconscious when I deal with them. I'm not good at talking. And especially, I'm not good at asking for things like money," admitted this tall, lanky, thirty-six-year-old African American, who had the quiet, disciplined look of a trusted doctor.

"Here's the thing." He leaned forward, bracing his elbows on his knees and pressing his palms together. "I know I'm good at

*what I do, and I know they want me, but all they offered was the minimum package." He ticked off the items on his fingers. "Entry-level salary, four weeks vacation, one week continuing medical education, and medical, dental, and retirement plans." **

Negotiation involves a proposal, or series of proposals, regarding what you want, coupled with how that will benefit the new organization.

Negotiating is not:
> A monologue.
> A battle of wits.
> A debate.
> A popularity contest.

And above all, negotiating is not a spontaneous event. It takes careful planning, and that begins before your initial interview. You will want to go after the highest possible salary both you and the job are worth. The actual figure is irrelevant. What matters is how you will stack up against your peers in terms of prestige and importance to the company. Make a point to find out what benefits the company has, and try to get yourself included in the highest-level ones you can possibly qualify for.

Send Up a Trial Balloon
Discuss Your Requirements

As you plan your own negotiating strategy, research the market value of your own skills by calling your trade association or looking in your trade publications. Contact employment agencies and executive recruiters. Ask others in the field about going rates. Make a trip to the library for books and magazine articles with detailed surveys listing current salaries by job description, experience level, and location. Check the Help Wanted ads. This will give you an idea of where the job you are looking at stands in relation to the rest in the field.

Strengthen your bargaining position by learning all you can about the job in relation to the company. During your initial interview, keep on the lookout for what's been happening in this position. Is the interim department head doing an acceptable job, or is the company getting desperate for a replacement? How long has the position been open? How often does it turn over? Have prior offers been made and turned down? What are the specific concerns of the organization and the interviewer? Your first interview should focus on gathering information about the company and selling yourself. Don't set up roadblocks. Once the company has decided to hire you, you can discuss the details.

Next, you must know what you want from the job offer. Don't think pie-in-the-sky, but rather ask yourself: "Based on what I know of the market and this company, what should I reasonably expect from this organization?" Be as objective as you can. Then ask yourself, "Why am I worth this?" It's not uncommon to have unrealistic expectations and exaggerated notions of your worth to potential employers, and a reality check about now is a good idea. To negotiate successfully, you must create a win-win situation and communicate the benefits of your proposal to the employer.

Once you've identified all the specific items you feel are appropriate, put them down in writing. This gives you a scorecard to use throughout the negotiating process that tells you what you've accomplished and what is still on the table.

At your final interview, raise the issues you've identified as important to you, and relate these to what the boss sees as valuable. Get a feel for what might and might not be acceptable.

* Dr. Bob had put a lot of thought into each of the items he wanted. He listed five:*
 1. Ten percent additional salary
 2. Two additional weeks vacation
 3. One additional week continuing medical education
 4. Two years paid malpractice insurance
 5. Training in microscopic surgery

"I've been thinking about this move for over a year," Dr. Bob replied. "I've had an eye open for opportunities listed in my medical journals, and before I came out here for the interview, I

did some checking around locally. As far as salary goes, the offer is about right for an entry-level person with no experience, but I spent four years as a resident at Cook County Hospital in Chicago. I think that puts me at least one step beyond entry level," he insisted. He knew the stress level he had experienced in Chicago and felt the extra vacation time was necessary to alleviate that. The malpractice insurance and continuing education were not unusual perks.

But it was the microscopic surgery that was especially important to him.

"I didn't even bring it up at the interview. I was just into reacting to their questions, and I was too nervous to even mention it." He paused. "One of the reasons this invitation excites me is that one of the associates is perfecting a microscopic surgery technique that is way beyond what anyone else is doing here. If I could just train under him...," his fingers itched in anticipation. *

Salaries are often the least negotiable, but benefits, personal time, parking, education, bonuses, and moving costs are all fair game. (You'll find a more complete list of commonly negotiated items at the end of this chapter.)

Remember, most employers offer new hires the minimal financial and benefits package they can get by with. And why not? It makes good business sense for the employer. You need to ask yourself if it makes good business sense for you. From your research, identify what is acceptable and what you want changed. Note what is acceptable, what is out of the question, and what is still possible and/or important to you.

Put Your Terms on the Table
Presenting Your Plan

The employer will try to make the job offer a one-time event. But once the offer has been made, you need to evaluate it against your requirements. Don't be afraid to ask for what you feel you're worth, as long as it's within generally accepted limits for your age and experience. Many employers are reluctant to negotiate salaries upward prior to seeing you perform, but remember your strongest bargaining position is before you say "yes" and that subsequent raises and bonuses are likely to be based on this first figure.

> *Saying what he wanted and actually moving forward with his proposals were two entirely different things. Just thinking about a confrontation made him break out in a nervous sweat. Yet he knew from experience that accepting the first offer without question would leave him with the uncomfortable feeling he had been taken advantage of. Now he felt his requests were reasonable, and his goal of training with the surgeon was too important to his future to let it slip away by default.*
>
> *In his written response to the offer, Dr. Bob began by stressing his interest in the position. He next indicated there were several matters he would like to discuss with the senior partners.* *

Thank You, But May We Talk Some More?
Introduce the Remaining Topics

Respond to any offer in writing. Establish as quickly as possible your desire to accept the position. This is key to any successful negotiation. Also establish quickly the parts of the offer you will accept and agree to. Then carefully state your desires. Do not discuss why you want them. At this initial stage, you just need to let them know what you want. When you meet with the principals, all of these will be negotiable and open for discussion. The outcome will depend on the acceptability of your reasoning and the flexibility of the employer. Your reasons for the requests will generate dialogue and discussion during your next meeting.

Identify Your Allies
Who Will Make the Decision?

Now identify who in the organization can make the changes you want to come about. It probably isn't the personnel department. Is it the person who interviewed you? Is it the direct supervisor, if that is someone different? Is it someone higher up? If you are working with a recruiter or employment agency, use them to feel out the company as to how much negotiating room there is. It's possible the employer has some hard constraints in some areas and flexibility in others. As you respond in writing to this initial offer, be sure your requests are within the realm of possibility for the company. Ask that the decision makers be present at the next interview.

"Who actually made you the offer?" I asked.
"The Personnel Director," he replied.
*"The Personnel Director won't have the authority to change anything. Why don't you set your agenda down in a memo and recommend the full partners review it?" ***

Preparation, practice, and presentation are the keys to successful negotiating. You will need to be prepared to present your requirements with enough information about yourself and your qualifications to justify your request. The employer assumes you are a hard worker and that you learn quickly, so these arguments won't get you much. It is paramount that you prepare your materials, arguments, and strategies in a manner that stresses the potential benefits to the organization. You must convince the interviewer that your unique experience and/or expertise will benefit the company more than any other candidate. Strengthen your position by quantifying those benefits in terms of dollars, either earned or saved. Put your reasoning down on paper. This clarifies your thinking.

*I now asked Dr. Bob to outline for himself a script consisting of point-by-point justification for his requests. This gave him the psychological lift he needed to overcome the lack of confidence in his communication skills and created a "comfort zone" for conversation during his meetings with the partners. ***

Now is the time to practice your presentation, much as you did for the initial interview. Making yourself comfortable with your presentation is even more important now.

When you meet with the decision makers, reiterate your desire to accept the position and outline those parts of the offer you both agree on. Remind them of your qualifications. Remember that demonstrated experience and tested skills count for a whole lot more than potential or promise. Through your presentation, you will want to alert and excite the employer with your potential, but your agenda should keep focused on the solid evidence of your current worth.

This additional information gives you control over the agenda during the meeting. It helps the organization decide the merits of your requirements and gives you a certain amount of leverage. W hen you are in the driver's seat, it's easier to communicate your confidence in yourself. This in turn affects how others perceive you.

The three senior partners agreed to meet with Dr. Bob. His initial excitement dissipated when they totally stonewalled him on the salary issue.

"We think this is a fair starting salary for a new person entering our practice," Dr. Noland, the spokesman, told the young physician following his presentation. "And six weeks vacation is just too much," He shook his head. "However, we are prepared to extend your continuing medical education benefit an additional two weeks."

They also offered to pay his malpractice insurance the first year.

*"But we don't see the value of training a second microsurgery specialist at this time," Dr. Noland concluded. ***

What Have You Gained? What Have You Lost?
Evaluating the Counteroffer

Once a counteroffer has been made, regroup. First, look at the points the company agreed to. Again, list the points still to be resolved. Evaluate the offer carefully. Sometimes, your needs will be met, but not in the form originally requested. You need to assess exactly what an alternative does for you.

Back in my office, I pointed out to a discouraged Dr. Bob that all was not lost and this was not necessarily their final offer, nor was it his.

Dr. Bob accepted this intellectually, but internally, his stress level soared. He waffled between his adamant position to continue the process and his fear that he had nuked the entire deal.

He needed patience, stress management, and a certain amount of plain old courage to get him through. Throughout college, Dr. Bob had been a long-distance runner. I encouraged him to take this up again to decrease the stress, but the courage would have to come from Dr. Bob's own conviction of his agenda.

When Dr. Bob took a second look at the offer from a calmer perspective, he could see progress.

"Picking up the malpractice insurance will save me $20,000 the first year," he admitted. "I guess I can accept the salary. I can put the difference toward my student loans, which I was worried about to begin with."

"I know you're disappointed they won't look at more vacation time, but," I pointed out, "two extra weeks for continuing medical education effectively adds two more weeks away from the stress of the office."

*He nodded in agreement. ***

Learn to view the negotiating process in a detached, analytical, unemotional way. Regard the rejection of any of your original demands impersonally, not as an individual slight. Continue to concentrate on how what you want benefits the organization, and how you will make a difference. Focus your justifications on your interests in the work, not on the position, salary, or benefits to you. Generate lots of possibilities for accomplishing your desires before issuing the "bottom line ultimatum." When you develop possible solutions, you present yourself as a creative problem solver with vision. You become an active participant in your own career future.

* For the next week, we focused on Dr. Bob's counteroffer: what he was gong to present to the partners and how he was going to present it in a way that demonstrated value to the group. Again, I asked him to do this in writing. Here is his working list. From this he developed his comments for the next meeting.

1. *This specialization is new and unique to this area. In all probability, new clients will be generated above and beyond what can be handled by Dr. Abbott, the current specialist, alone.*

2. *It is also a high-profit procedure, and a second specialist will be able to produce significant additional revenue.*
3. *A generation exists between Dr. Abbott and me. By the time I finish my training and develop a reputation in the specialty, he will be approaching retirement. When he does, you'll have to replace him. If I'm already on board and trained, there'll be no need for an expensive and time-consuming recruitment effort.*
4. *I have been successful in my previous medical training. My academic and surgical expertise demonstrated this during my residency. ★*

Head 'Em Off at the Pass and Call in the Big Guns
Identify the Road Blocks

At this stage, you must identify any stumbling blocks. Use your resources, and contact all potential allies to address and overcome these. Ask your references to contact decision makers. If you have contacts within the organization, explore how they can help you. Your job now is to provide as many answers as you can to the questions you know will come up, covering as many "what ifs" and "yes, buts" as you can think of.

★ When Dr. Bob and I met again, we were coming down to the wire. We looked at what he needed to do to increase his acceptability to the partners. Now was the time to enlist his allies in the medical group. Dr. Bob had spoken to Dr. Abbott, the specialist, as soon as the firm had expressed an interest in him. Dr. Abbott had agreed to take him on as an intern, providing Dr. Bob could convince the partners to accept the arrangement. Now Dr. Bob solicited his active support, asking him to speak to the partners on his behalf.

Dr. Bob met with the surgical specialist and gave him a list of the points he had previously made. He asked him to speak to the partners as soon as possible so that when they met the following week with Dr. Bob they would have as much time as possible to consider the specialist's input before coming to their decision. ★

225

The bottom line for the employer is still getting the best person for the least amount of dollars or the least amount of hassle. Keep the discussion focused on the benefits to the company.

Dr. Bob needed to convince the partners he was worth the extras he was asking for—that it was in their best interest to consider his request. All the while, he continued to stress his interest in joining this particular practice. Dr. Bob accurately perceived the hostility of one of the partners. He needed to turn him around.

We took a determined look at what this doctor might be reacting to. Dr. Bob felt that to the doctor he appeared to be a pretentious young upstart right out of medical school who had an inflated opinion of his worth. To change his mind, Dr. Bob needed to convince him of the positive benefits his experience would bring to the firm.

"Why not take the bull by the horns," I suggested. "Ask for a meeting and get to know him on a one-to-one basis."

Because of the hostility, Dr. Bob hesitated. He was sure the doctor would have nothing to do with him. And even if he did, he wasn't sure he was up to the confrontation. On the other hand, I pointed out, nothing ventured, nothing gained. To his surprise the doctor accepted his invitation for lunch. They met the following day, and Dr. Hollister spoke quite candidly.

"You impress me as an arrogant opportunist. Don't you think you're being presumptuous?" he asked flat out.

"Not really, sir," Dr. Bob began, his stomach rebelling against the antagonism. It was too late to leave, so he might as well tough it out and give it his best shot, he thought.

"The pace, the variety, and the volume of cases I handled in Chicago place me in more than an entry-level category. I proved my worth there, and I bring this experience to your practice. I appreciate all you have agreed to so far. I have some heavy educational debts. They run in the neighborhood of $100,000, and they trouble me. My family was very supportive when I went to medical school, but not in a financial way. My student loans are coming due in the next four years, and I won't default on them."
He paused a moment, then looked up, grinned and added, "My father would kill me." He then turned to the key subject.

"It's the opportunity of working with Dr. Abbott that makes joining this practice so important to me. His technique has fascinated me since I first read about it in the JAMA journal at school. This technology will help solve a number of medical problems in their early stages. That's what really excites me."

The doctor came away with a better understanding of Dr. Bob's position and confirmed that he was the holdout. Although making no commitment, he assured Dr. Bob he would take this new information into consideration.

"By and large, I feel this is a good match," Dr. Bob began the next meeting with the partners. "I am deeply convinced the expertise I developed during my Cook County Hospital residency will strengthen this practice."

After he had stressed the matters he felt they agreed on, he pressed on to the one unresolved item, the one of primary importance to him: A one-year training program with Dr. Abbott.

"I know I will personally gain a great deal from this," he acknowledged.

"Now let's consider it from your side of the table. I believe you are risking very little in allowing me to do this," and he outlined why he felt this would benefit the entire practice, using the working list he developed earlier. "I believe what I am asking has only positive outcomes for everyone," he reiterated.

The meeting ended with the partners appearing fairly comfortable that they were reaching common ground but feeling they needed to discuss his interest in training for this specialization with other members of the staff, before making a final offer the following week.

When the panel met with Dr. Bob, the meeting was short and to the point.

"This is what we are offering you. Please review it, and give us your decision on Friday," Dr. Noland told him. *

When the final offer is made, you may either accept or reject. Look it over carefully to ensure that you are making the right decision.

* "Man-o-man, will you look at this?" I could see he was pleased with himself as he handed me the proposal.

227

The offer included the original salary and vacation, the additional two weeks of continuing education, and the first year's premium on his malpractice insurance. The partners had finally agreed to the training program, based on Dr. Abbott's recommendation and support, but only after Dr. Bob had worked six months as a general surgeon, the position originally offered. For the next eighteen months, he would spend 50 percent of his time with the specialist as his assistant, learning the new surgical technique. Following that, if he passed the qualifying exam, he was to commit to remaining with the partnership for a minimum of two more years, when he would be considered for an associate partnership.

"This is really excellent. You've done a great job," I congratulated him.

"All I need to do now is sign and return it."

"Not so fast!" I cautioned. *

Put It in Writing
Follow Up

If you accept the offer, make sure you understand exactly what you are going to commit to. It's in your best interest to be responsible for coming up with the final draft of what you believe has been decided. Then, if there is some misunderstanding, the employer must come to you for clarification, as opposed to you going to them. The ball is now in their court, where it should be.

* *"In some of our first discussions you told me that independence was an important value to you. I feel it is crucial for you to recognize that you are essentially committing yourself to that organization for four years: six months of full-time general surgery, plus the eighteen months of training in the specialization and an additional two years after that."*

Dr. Bob needed to see that although he had been offered much of what he wanted, there were strings attached, and he needed to be comfortable with those strings if the partners were going to make this considerable investment of time, energy, training, and money.

228

"Yes, I think this is an offer I can live with," he told me the next day. *"It is a four-year commitment. It means putting off my own private practice for at least that long. And if I decide on that, I'll have to practice somewhere else. That's part of the package, too. They don't want to train a competitor. On the other hand, in one way or another, I've got everything I asked for, and in the case of the training, even more. I would say this is very fair, very fair indeed. In four years, I might find a partnership offer very desirable."* *

Negotiations eventually boil down to a matter of two or three meetings in which you give and take; you win some, you lose some, and at some point you come to a middle ground. At this time, you have to agree or disagree. Nine times out of ten, you will get some of what you ask for. Now you either accept the employment and terms you've agreed upon so far, or you don't, in which case you thank them very much for their thoughtful consideration and move on with your life.

* Dr. Bob called Dr. Noland, thanked him for the offer, and said he was accepting it. He told him he would be submitting the offer as he understood it in writing, so that if there was any misunderstanding it could be cleared up immediately.

We drafted the acceptance letter and sent it over by messenger that day. The partners reviewed it and agreed as it was presented. The contract was drawn up accordingly. When it was signed, all parties walked away feeling that although each had given some, each had made an excellent deal. *

Common Negotiable Items

A signing bonus
An annual performance bonus
Bonus program based on meeting specific performance goals
A severance settlement
The right to do freelance work on your own time
Cost of moving
Low-interest loans
Company-paid pension plan
Paid-up life insurance
Health club, country club, and/or private club membership
Service and professional club memberships
First-class air travel
Airline VIP clubs
Extra vacation time
Sabbatical leaves
Annual physical examination
Child care/parental leave
Personal time
Education
Stock options
A larger or better office
A reserved place in the company parking lot
Deferred compensation
A company car
Reimbursement for entertaining at home
Expense account
Flexible work schedule
Part-time/job sharing
Retirement plans
Profit sharing
Paid trips

*

"I think most of us are looking for a calling, not a job." — Studs
Terkel

*

"Work is much more fun than fun." — *Noel Coward*

*

*"Career and identity are inextricably bound up: Indeed they are
almost equivalent."* — *Douglas LaBier*

*

*"The policeman is the little boy who grew up to be what he said he
was going to be."* —*Raymond Burr*

*

11   Establishing Your Time Line
Setting a Realistic Schedule

"Risk is the price of admission as you begin your search for a more fulfilling career."

Whenever you launch a new job search, it is important to establish a realistic time line. To imagine that you will find the job of your dreams before the rent comes due is not only unrealistic, it sets you up for failure—definitely a blow, often a crippling one, to your self-esteem. Each step takes time and therefore patience. If each is done thoroughly, you will position yourself not only for this career change, but for all future moves.

Begin this process of career exploration gently. "Think of your career as a journey of discovery, not a climb up some organizational ladder," suggest Stephen M. Polan and Mark Levine in *Worth* magazine. "There's no predetermined path. Your career is a series of moves from project to project, employer to employer, even industry to industry. Each project should be exciting to contemplate."

Talk with people, volunteer your time, or take on an internship in an industry that interests you. Ask to tag along with someone for a day at his or her job, and observe the actual operation of the occupation. It's paramount that this step in the process be approached cautiously and with time for reflection. It may take a number of forays into different industries or employment situations before you can comfortably decide on one.

When I first moved to Santa Barbara, I interned with an art gallery. I had a fantasy of owning and operating my own gallery. Three weeks into the internship, it was clear I was not interested, nor did I have the personality for the management functions of ownership, much less the skills to handle the financial aspects. I was attracted to the glamour of owning an art gallery, not the reality of the business. When my internship ended, I happily regressed to being an admirer of art and remain so to this day. That was a reality check, and it is a very important aspect of decision making for people making mid-life career changes.

As with other areas in our lives, there are no guarantees in this process. You simply put forth your best effort, weigh your options, and then decide.

Figler suggests that 80 percent of your work will consist of "detective work" or "behind the scenes" work to establish a foundation for a successful career change and job search. As we have often said before, research is the key. Much of this involves reading books, magazines, newspapers, and employee literature to establish a frame of reference for determining where to place your focus.

You will also spend time on self-discovery. When I work with individual clients through the Personal Assessment phase, I require them to keep a career journal and regularly record their thoughts regarding the process and what they are learning about themselves. All of this culminates in the realization of a new persona, your Professional Self.

It is important that you do take the time to incorporate all aspects of this process. Your long-term goal is not just to find another job, but to establish your Professional Self through this self-discovery process. This often involves changes in your basic attitude about yourself as a working person. A positive attitude lets you ask, "What opportunities does this current situation present that the old one didn't?" In this economy, there are far more opportunities to become your own boss, to turn your interests and hobbies into money-making ventures, and to develop areas of knowledge that give you additional opportunities in the future. There are numerous free ways to learn things, either through adult education classes or university programs online. You have to change your idea of education coming from an institution to the idea of learning by whatever means is most appropriate for you and your career needs. Many professional organizations have annual meetings that are excellent places to network, get caught up on the latest trends in your profession, check out the job openings in the on-site career center, and maybe dance foolishly in the bar until 2 a.m. (I digress…oops…sorry). You can hear deans of graduate schools talk about their programs and what the profession values as scholarship. You can talk to graduate students as they leave these academic programs ready to tackle the problems they came here to solve, filled with optimism and good ideas. Suffice to say, professional conferences are where you need to be if you are looking for an infusion of information about the career you are considering.

If, somewhere throughout this process, you need help gaining perspective or with an attitude adjustment, seek the help of career professionals. They can help you process your options, as well as your fears, anger, and all the other emotions that play a critical role in this effort. This job market is not for sissies or the unprepared. Do your homework. Ask for help. Consider your options. Then proceed.

As you progress, you will also develop a new, updated vocabulary for describing yourself in the world of work. This vocabulary will sound more fluent, descriptive, and authentic as you move along.

You probably won't notice these changes at first, but as a career counselor I can assure you that I quickly begin to hear these changes in my clients' descriptions of themselves. I see ongoing evidence of their taking control, of feeling more powerful, of becoming more sophisticated job searchers. After perhaps weeks of what looks to you like unproductive effort, suddenly you become aware that you are making more knowledgeable decisions about the direction your career is taking. You see how best to use your time in each aspect of the process and to look forward to a time when the process will come to a successful conclusion.

To help you gauge yourself, take a look at the suggested time lines at the end of this chapter. The first sets the pace if you are exploring a new career; the second, if change has found you and your first priority, is immediate employment.

Don't Jump Ship
Employed People Make Stronger Candidates

If you are employed, I encourage you to stay that way until you've accepted another offer. It's difficult to look for work when you are holding down another job, but it's infinitely harder if you're without a paycheck. Unemployment not only brings about its own stress, it encourages you to rush the process. If you are unhappy where you are, try to restructure the job as best you can to minimize the bad and maximize the good. Look closely at personality styles (Chapter 5) for some suggestions.

The other advantage to being employed is that interviewers tend to look upon the employed as seeking new opportunities and the unemployed as desperate for work.

Help Is Out There
From the Feds to Your Next-Door Neighbor

And then there's the money part. If you've been laid off, your first agenda item is a trip to the nearest state employment office. Not only will you register for unemployment insurance, but you'll file a job application that will be entered into your state's system. California's Job Match system, for instance, is a statewide computer network matching vacancies with suitable applicants locally, regionally, and statewide. The Kansas Job Service offers two-day job search workshops, as well as one-on-one vocational counseling and aptitude testing. Your next step is to visit any federal training or jobs programs in your area, such as the Job Training Network. Both state and federal programs often offer job search workshops that can be very helpful as well.

For the worker displaced by "downsizing," the feds fund programs under the Economically Displayed Workers Assistance Act. In California, under this program, some thirty Experience Unlimited job clubs have been established by the California Employment Development Department. Restricted to those with two years of college or equivalent education and those looking for technical, management, or other professional employment, the clubs act essentially as a member-operated employment agency.

Uncle Sam isn't your only source of help. The American Association of Retired Persons offers AARP WORKS, a series of eight workshops on employment planning for older adults. Forty Plus is another self-help organization for professional and managerial employees age forty and older.

If you have a computer and an online service, check out the career and job search forums. You can list your résumé, review employers looking for new people, ask questions on a forum, and get free information on résumé writing and interviewing techniques. You'll also find a number of publications and services available for a fee. Once you have determined the Internet is a fruitful venue for your search, there are a number of books, as well as how-to seminars, available.

Now is the time to network big time. Jack Erdlen, chief executive officer of The Erdlen Bograd Group, an outplacement and human resource resources consulting firm headquartered in Wellesley, Massachusetts, suggests you begin by making a list of everyone you know. And I mean everyone—from the CEO's you've worked with, to your clergyman, to the person you buy your burgers from. Then sort them in the most likely order of "hearing about jobs" and start making those contacts.

Next, you must look to your budget. List your mortgage or rent payment, utilities, insurance, car loan, food, gasoline, and job-hunting costs. Pay only these, advocates twice-fired Jane Bryant Quinn. Put your other bills in a box marked "later," she says. Next, add up your income. If there is a gap, see how long your cash reserves will last. Consider a home-equity loan to give yourself some extra cash. "Your goal is to cover basic expenses for at least nine months while you hunt for work," she advises.

Watch out for rip-offs. Résumé writing, job-hunting services, and the like can come at a high price with little results. Check out exactly what you are buying before you plunk down those precious dollars. If you decide to hire a consultant, the best way to do so is armed with references from colleagues or friends. Even then, make sure you ask lots of questions. Meanwhile, check out your nearest adult education center and your alumni career center.

"Always ask: 'What concrete, in-hand materials will I be provided with and what knowledge will I walk away with?'" advises Benita Ugoline, owner of Career Architect, a job-search training company.

It is important that you give yourself the time and mental energy it takes to identify, search out, and land a new job. Although a great deal of your efforts now will be active rather than introspective, it is a good time to take stock, by necessity perhaps rather than choice, of the things that will be important for you to consider as you look for a new job.

To cover the cash-flow gap and abate your stress, look for part-time work. It's often easier to get, and it allows you time to pursue more substantial full-time work. Today, even professionals are getting into the act. Interim, a fort Lauderdale, Florida–based temporary agency, offers temporary doctors, lawyers, paralegals, accountants, and other skilled professionals, at wages as high as $75.00 an hour. By taking a temporary assignment, you will still be a member of the workforce, but your part-time status will be a constant reminder that this is only temporary. Your long-range goal is full-time employment.

The Awful Truth
There Ain't No Free Lunch

Changing careers requires thought and courage, and should not be entered into lightly. One of the realities of moving from a field where you have proved yourself to something entirely different is that you are not likely to receive your old salary. Sometimes, you need to sacrifice in the short term in order to realize your maximum long-range potential. Can you live with what you are offered?

* Ellie Fairchild came back to see me when she received the job offer from a Nevada radio station.

"Congratulations. It looks like you've done just exactly what you set out to do."

"Yes, that's true," she admitted. "But there is a downside."

"Oh?"

"My salary will be about half of what I made at the department store."

"A hard choice, but not at all unusual," I assured her.

Ellie spent some time thoroughly reviewing and evaluating her options. She decided to accept the job, but not without some stomach fluttering and finger crossing.

Her gamble paid off. Within three years, she had achieved her old salary level. She felt professionally satisfied and fulfilled. *

Allow yourself time to seek advice, venture into new areas, mull over your options, and eliminate those that no longer meet your requirements. Seek out job fairs. Offer potential employers a copy of your résumé. Give them a bit of background on yourself, and ask lots of questions. Find out all you can. Send thank-you notes to everyone who gives you the time of day.

Trial and error are good teachers. Chances are the first career change you decide upon will not turn out. It is usually the third or fourth option you explore that turns out to be the best. Don't despair; your work on the ones you discard is part of the process and is in no way a waste of time!

Kevin Avalos had worked in the computer information system of the banking industry for ten years. He felt unfulfilled and couldn't see himself in banking for the rest of his work life.

The first interest area he explored involved working in the training and development department of an organization providing in-house seminars to employees. He liked the idea of more contact with people, of being an expert, and of providing a service. After extensive library research, conducting informational interviews, and actually going to three job interviews, he realized that although he liked the majority of the work, he did not look forward to the notion of being "on stage" every day, as he would be in a seminar atmosphere.

His second search took him into the area of consulting, with emphasis on his computer expertise, but again this was too much like what he was doing at the bank. While exploring this area, he interned with a consultant who had been hired by an accounting firm to upgrade its computer system. Kevin found himself attracted to the accounting field and began the process of retraining to support a change in that direction. By this time, he had accepted a transfer by the bank to a smaller community. As he continued his accounting preparation, he developed an internship with a major accounting firm in his new community during tax season. Because of the size of the community, the accounting firm was smaller than he would have considered in his old neighborhood. This gave him the opportunity to work closely with the principals of the firm, and conversely, for them to observe him at close range. They were impressed with what they saw and offered him a full time position. They even agreed to give him time off to prepare for the Certified Public Accountant exam.

It took Kevin two full years to move from computers to accounting. During that time, he continued his job at the bank and explored his options in the evenings and on weekends. Exploring the two aborted areas gave him confidence that accounting was the best career choice for him at this point in his life. He was able to pinpoint just exactly what he wanted from his new career: the opportunity to demonstrate expertise in a highly technical and specialized area, and to work independently while allowing contact with clients and co-workers as the need arose. *

At This Point in Time
Determining Where You Are and What You Need to Do

You may not need to go through the entire Professional Self Model because you come to it having done some work already. The joy of this model is that you can enter from any place you happen to be along the career development continuum.

Some aspects will take longer than others, depending on where you are. Reentry people, for example, usually need a great deal of emphasis on the Personal Assessment section. People who have significant work experience in one career area and are now changing directions usually need very little time on this because they are fairly clear on their values, interests, and skills. Their emphasis will be on the research portion of the model.

If returning to a formal program is not reasonable, either for financial or time constraints, explore evening extension programs at your nearest university or college. Many offer certificate programs at a fraction of the time and cost of an additional degree. Some professional associations also offer training and certificate programs. Look for computer training through adult education programs or your local computer store.

For every job seeker and career changer, now is a good time to review your skills and identify those that need updating. Middle managers may need to learn new leadership styles. Engineers must become more "human"; humanists must become more technically literate. Everyone must be competent with the tools of the computing and advanced telecommunications age. The global economy calls for all of us to enter into an international dialogue where we learn about each other and our ways so that we can better understand the world we live in.

Your marketing tools will need reworking, since with each new job search you will want your résumé and all other marketing tools to conform to the new position.

Checkpoint Charlie
Keeping Yourself on Track

As you begin this career change process, it is essential to set some obvious checkpoints along the way. Once a month, you should evaluate what you've accomplished. Try writing a statement at the beginning of each month on the current status of your career search, and then articulate what it is you want to achieve during the next month. Put that statement in an envelope and seal it. At the end of the month, write another statement about what you have learned and what your attitude is about the process. Compare the two documents, and decide your level of progress. How committed are you to career change? Did you work as hard as you intended? Are you frustrated because the answers are not coming as easily as you thought they would? Are you clearer about your Professional Self? These statements not only serve as performance indicators but also help you pinpoint problem areas.

You may be asking yourself to do too much too soon. You may be overwhelmed with the process. But don't think about giving up. As I stress throughout this book, the kind of change you want to occur does not happen without planning and participation on your part. Finding meaningful work does not "happen" to you; it is a matter of making it "happen" for yourself. So set reasonable, measurable, time-limited goals, and evaluate them on a regular basis. Look for ways to make it fun.

Keep in mind as we talk about change that change is often resisted, typically because people do not feel they have the skills to deal with the new situation. Be patient. Keep going. You are gaining those skills.

Another aspect of any change is the element of risk: risk of failure, risk you will be disappointed in yourself, risk of unforeseen factors and events. Don't let this stop you. Risk is the price of admission as you begin your search for a more fulfilling career.

This is the only way you will find out what you have to offer and how much value your work has for others. If you look upon this change as an opportunity, as you go on you can expect to feel curiosity, challenge, and hopefulness. Stress, helplessness, and fragmentation will give way to new creativity, control, and commitment.

If you start your career search by identifying your skills and incorporate all of the components of the Professional Self Model outlined here, your realistic time line for landing a position that meets your needs ranges from eighteen to twenty-four months. If you are unemployed with job search as your number-one priority, a commonly accepted rule of thumb is that it will take one month for every $10,000 of salary you expect. The general economy and the industry base of the community you are in will also affect the time it takes for you to be successful. This time line can be shortened if you are working with a career counselor or with a career development group, such as a job club, that will help you monitor your progress and offer advice on shortcuts with the process.

To ensure the success of your career search, it must be incorporated into your everyday life. If you are working on this while holding down a full-time job, plan on spending no more than two hours a day on your career change. If you are already pounding the pavement, dedicating four hours a day is a better goal, but certainly no more than six. The main thing is to commit to spending a specific amount of time every day at this. Actively engaging yourself in this process will enhance your chances of success and will minimize the time it takes to move from the first steps of the search to accepting a new position.

Work smarter, not harder. Assess how much of this process you are comfortable doing yourself and how much can be done more comfortably or efficiently with the assistance of professionals. Investing in professional career counseling or taking a career search class through your local adult education program may be the best way to overcome personal inertia and ensure an in-depth completion of each task. Being accountable to another is often the push you need to keep you on your schedule. You also get feedback from people who are not closely invested in your career search. This can be very helpful because it is sometimes difficult to get an objective opinion from people who are close to you. Outsiders can often shed a guiding light when you reach a stalemate.

All Work and No Play Makes You-Know-What
Take Time to Smell the Flowers

Make this search a part of your life, but not all of your life. This is important. Relax, continue your normal routine, but adjust it to incorporate the time needed to conduct a thorough career search. Do not compromise other important aspects of your life, like exercise, during this time. Physical activity is an excellent way to relive the inevitable stress that builds up. Keep up your social life as well. Friends are especially important at this time.

Reward yourself for small accomplishments, and acknowledge the big ones with hats and horns! You are making a big move in your life, and this should not be done without some degree of acknowledgment and ceremony.

Try to find a balance between having the patience to let things happen and taking the initiative so things will happen. Every job search calls for a readjustment in this equation, and only through trial and error can you establish this balance.

As you have seen through the friends you have met within these pages, each step takes patience and determination. But all of these colleagues persevered, went head to head with their own fears, addressed the barriers that stood in the way, and accomplished their personal goals. They are living proof that the process works, that this investment in yourself pays off. If you haven't already, start today. As you define, refine, and establish your Professional Self, you'll know you're worth it!

Estimated Time Line for Career Changers

I. **Months 1 to 4**
   Goals: Assessment/Education/Information
   Activities to consider during this time:
   1. Explore career counseling.
   2. Consider career change courses available through adult education or a college or university in your area.
   3. If you are on your own, work through the exercises on interests, personality styles, and values and get to know your Professional Self.
   4. Carefully catalog your skills and choose those you want to carry forward, those you need to acquire.
   5. Identify people who will be supportive of your idea of career change; look to them for comfort, encouragement, and advice. Beware of those who may try to sabotage your plans. Remember, not everyone likes change for themselves, and these people are not willing to encourage it in others.
   6. Establish your personal network.
   7. Develop a reading list of books and magazines that increases your knowledge of careers and job market predictions. Now is the time to meet the reference librarian at your local library who knows where all the good books are located. Frequent the career and business sections of your local book store, and create your own career library.
   8. Read your reading list!
   9. Develop a list of possible careers you are willing to consider.
   10. Develop your job search strategies, and learn how to look for the work you want.

II. **Months 5 to 10**
   Goals: Investigation/Risk-taking/Elimination
   Activities to consider during this time:
   1. Informational interviews
   2. Active networking within the professional communities you have identified
   3. Résumé development
   4. Application to viable career positions
   5. Mock interviews
   6. Follow up as necessary with career counselor and/or support people
   7. Elimination and reestablishment of career categories as they surface

III. **Months 11 to 24**
   Goals: Actual career change
   Activities to consider during this time:
   1. Through process of elimination, identify career area and positions of choice.
   2. Identify concrete steps to move you in that direction.
      a. Retraining
      b. Internships
      c. Skill building
   3. Make connections with people and places that provide experiences to make you employable in your new career.
   4. Apply for positions.
   5. Interview.
   6. Review offers.
   7. Negotiate salary and benefits.
   8. Accept most suitable offer.
   9. Thank your support system.
   10. Celebrate!
   11. Repeat as often as necessary.

Estimated Time Line for Active Job Seekers

I.   **Month 1**
      Goals: Motivation/Prioritization/Temporary employment
      Activities to consider during this time:
      1.   Contact the personnel office of your former (or soon to be former) employer.
            a.   Inquire as to whether outplacement services are available.
            b.   Ask about the procedure for unemployment benefits.
            c.   Ask about status of benefits as a result of the layoff.
            d.   Visit your local state employment office and your local federal jobs/training programs.
      2.   Assess your financial needs to maintain as familiar a lifestyle as possible. You may need help from a financial planner or a career counselor for a realistic look at this.
      3.   Based on this information, if immediate employment is your first priority in order to meet monthly expenses, rework your résumé.
      4.   Contact professional search firms and temporary agencies in your area with your résumé, and let them know you are available. Check out the Help Wanted sections of area newspapers and professional journals.
      5.   Enlist your support system to help you with mock interviews with immediate part-time employment in mind. (This instantly identifies you as a skilled and talented job seeker, which gives you the psychological lift you need at this point, and it helps overcome the immediate feeling of panic.)
      6.   Contact the local Chamber of Commerce for economic forecasts and a copy of the business directory in your community to determine what you have to work with in terms of potential employers.
      7.   Schedule at least four, but no more than six, hours a day actively seeking employment.

8.   Refer to Career Change Time Line, and incorporate initial activities into your schedule.

II.   Months 2 and 3

Goals: Establishment of contacts/Job interviews/Maintenance of motivation and self-esteem
Activities to consider during this time:

1. Continue to use your support system in the job search arena.
2. Conduct mailings to family and friends enlisting their help in your search; include specific goals and employment agendas.
3. Follow up with phone calls requesting names of potential contacts and employment leads.
4. Continue to polish your résumé and interviewing skills as job search becomes more clearly defined.
5. Build into your day a way to have fun and relieve stress.
6. Continue to maintain contacts with professional search firms, responding to their leads with applications and informational interviews.
7. Continue with activities from Career Change Time Line.

III.   Months 4 to 6

Goals: Evaluation of employment status/Changing gears/Full-time professional employment
Activities to consider during this time:

1. Continue with activities from Career Change Time Line.
2. Continue to pursue employment opportunities as they arise through your use of search firms, family and friends, and leads you obtain through your own research.
3. If full-time employment has not been offered by now, take stock of the situation and determine whether you need to switch gears. Are you fishing where the fish are? Do you need to find another pond? Do you have the right bait?

4. Work closely with your career support system to fine-tune your strategy and validate that you are doing all you can at this time. Make adjustments as necessary until you are successful.
5. Evaluate offers.
6. Negotiate salary and benefits.
7. Accept position.
8. Thank your support system.
9. Celebrate!
10. Repeat as often as necessary.

A   The Role of the Career Counselor
What to Expect

Although the majority of my professional experience has been with traditional-age college students, I also work privately with people my age who are emotionally mature, financially grounded, and willing—albeit timidly—to look seriously at career change. They are satisfied with what they have accomplished but are ready, or forced, to move on. Hardly anyone I know has escaped the downsizing of American enterprise. Many successful middle-aged people are taking stock and reordering the rhythm of their lives.

Most of these clients have never before sought the services of a career counselor and are unsure what to expect. Among their first questions is, "How long will it take?" One of my first challenges is to tell them that the answer to their search lies in a process and is not instantly available in some computer. They must learn to find the answers to their questions by using electronic communication, books, and magazines and by talking to actual people such as reference librarians. John Naisbitt, co-author of the popular *Megatrends* books, writes that the mark of an intelligent person at the beginning of the twenty-first century will not be the amount of information he or she knows, but rather his or her ability to access information.

I also give my clients materials to complete at home. These are assignments on values, interests, skills, and personality styles, much as you have done here. To do my job well, I need as much information as I can get from them. While they are collecting information, I am busy observing the process, taking note of the gaps and vulnerable areas of their plans, and assessing the reality of their choices. These career inventories and values exercises provide a point of departure from which we can begin the second phase of our time together.

Rethinking Your World
Act II

During this time, I see their spirits soar as they begin to see new career possibilities. My goal is to create a common knowledge base in order to make our communication more effective and to help put a different slant on their worldview. We get used to seeing the world through our own eyes and filtering information through our own unique circumstances. Before decisions are made about future career goals, it is important to take time to reeducate yourself about the world.

Bill Barnes stormed into my office, his demeanor daring me to disagree.

"There are no teaching jobs out there for someone with an English degree," he bellowed. "I've sent out a hundred applications, and there are no jobs!"

"Okay," I said. "Why don't you look for something else?"

He stopped in his tracks, and while he was getting his breath, I continued.

"You've done everything you could, and you've discovered there are no teaching jobs in English. Let's look at what other areas your education will take you." *

Career changers begin to see a number of options as we move into this new phase, which I refer to as the "career-of-the-week period," where they become aware of some not-so-obvious careers. Each session, they come in with a new plan based on their previous week's reading assignment or interview. This information has expanded their horizon and created a knowledge base from which their ideas and decisions can springboard. Now I can ask questions based on my observations.

As we establish common ground, the hard work starts. We begin to look at their need for change and at their support system. Why do they want to change careers? Can they articulate what they will miss about their current career? What five things are they proud of about their work? Who among their family or friends will be supportive? Who will sabotage their attempts to change? How will people react to them differently based on their new professional identity? How will it feel to not have the power an executive position involves? Will it be worth the less stressful work environment their new career might provide? Are they willing to relocate or take a cut in pay to establish themselves in a new field? How these questions are answered offers important insight into the clarity and conviction of clients, and how dedicated they are to actually making a change.

What my clients begin to realize is that they are changing not only their careers but their identities as well—the way they interact with the world and the way the world interacts with them. They also begin to realize that there are a number of fulfilling things they could do, and that it really does come down to choices, not just one single career. Now comes the realization that this idea of career change is not stagnant or a one-time event. It is fluid and, even more, it is a process of trial and error. As with most things in adult life, patience to allow things to happen is the cornerstone to successful career transitions. It now becomes clear why the earlier information gathering is so important. It reduces the risk of making a decision based on misinformation or lack of information.

As my clients become more skilled at this trial and error part of the process, our time together is coming to an end. They have a clearer vision of their experience and a more sophisticated knowledge base, and I have helped them with perspective and process. We often connect again later around job offers and negotiations strategies once they have settled into a new path.

*In Kevin's case, we met twice a month for the first four months. During this time, we worked through the Personal Assessment phase. He kept a career journal, and I assigned reading and research to expand his knowledge of career opportunities and of the job market. Once that was done, we both felt he could work effectively on his own, and we began a once-a-month schedule. He relocated soon after that, and he contacted me twice by letter with questions. Almost two years to the day after our first meeting, we met for the last time to discuss the negotiation of his salary and benefits for the accounting firm offer. *

Career changers often find the aid of a career counselor beneficial in this comprehensive planning process. Look for someone who has training, experience, and a track record. You'll find Certified Career Counselors listed in the Yellow Pages, or you can get the names of those in your area from the National Career Development Association. Your area colleges and universities are also another good source for references. My friends and clients continue to insist that this "taking stock" guides them into a more individualized career plan for themselves and for their future.

B   When and How to Use an Employment Agency

Employment agencies should be viewed as one of your marketing tools. Like reading the want ads, they may not produce the job for you, but you would be foolish to ignore them.

First, you should understand that all employment agencies are not the same. Some deal exclusively with temporary workers, others only with permanent placements, and some do a little of everything.

Downsizing has resulted in a burgeoning temporary worker industry, and one that is constantly changing. Part-time professionals totaled more than 4.7 million in 1994. Of these, 28 percent were men, and 61 percent were employed as engineers, computer scientists, natural scientists, health care providers, teachers, lawyers, and the like. Another 26 percent were employed in administrative and management-related occupations.

Temporary work can have several advantages. It can get you inside companies where the unadvertised jobs are; you can try out jobs and fields before making a commitment; you can learn what "cutting-edge" companies are doing in your field. You can acquire and refine practical or technical skills. Temporary work allows you to beef up your résumé as you gain valuable work experience.

Like everything else these days, temporary agencies generally specialize in certain types of workers. Some handle only the traditional temporary worker, filling in for sick or vacationing employees or to get rid of a temporary backlog. These jobs are still worth looking at. You'll be getting a paycheck, which will ease the pressure to take just any job. You'll be getting recent experience. You'll be keeping your skills current. You'll get to try different working environments and different jobs. This can be a great place for entry-level workers, reentry people, and career changers to start and you'll get plenty of opportunities to practice your interviewing skills.

The downside is that the pay probably will not be much. Your stints tend to be brief, so the income will not necessarily be steady. These temporary jobs tend not to be at higher levels of expertise either, and few lead to permanent hires.

Temp-to-hire is a variation on this theme. In this case, if you and the employer are happy with each other after a stated time, you become their employee. These jobs can require more skills and experience. They also give you a chance to try out some options you might not have thought of.

Another form of temporary work is the job shop. These place experienced technical people in temporary situations, usually working on a specific project. Project durations vary, from a week or two, to a year or two.

Temporary work for the skilled professional can be attractive, up to $600 a day for top-level managers, although you probably won't get any benefits. However, as the temporary field becomes more permanent, even this is changing.

Employment agencies seek permanent placements. Job levels vary from entry level to highly skilled. These firms are hired by employers, who generally pay them. The jobs they refer you to will be those available at client firms. Although employment agencies are always aware of their applicant pool and keep their ears open for new opportunities, they generally do not go looking for openings outside their client base.

Executive search firms, or "headhunters," seek permanent placement for high-level positions, especially in upper management and the professional ranks. They also work with highly skilled technical people. Although these firms also work for employer clients, they will go beyond this base for a qualified candidate or someone with unique, hard-to-find skills.

Your telephone book will probably tell you which agencies do what. You'll want to interview several, and you can probably do some initial screening by phone. This is a good way to start, and you'll want to make an appointment with any that fit your needs.

Ask what types of people they specialize in placing. Each agency is different in its expertise. If they don't want to tell you this, ask how many placements they typically make in your field, advises Gary Kravetz, National Career Choices. Look for an agency with enough counselors to serve their applicants. You'll want someone with enough time to look for a suitable match between you and an employer.

Ask what testing and training programs are available. Some have extensive programs; some, virtually none. If programs are available, ask about fees. In fact, ask about fees in general. Some agencies are paid totally by employers; others are not. And there are a variety of fee structures.

You can expect the agency to review your résumé and make helpful comments. They'll also tell you where you can realistically find a job and give you some idea of the pay ranges in your field. Many will provide testing for specific job fields.

On your part, be flexible. Be willing to take some risk, advises Cris Wood, Western Staff Services. Be flexible both on salary issues and job descriptions. Be willing to try something out of your norm.

Keep in touch with your agencies; once a week is probably about right. Use as many as fit your needs. Each agency has a different client base, and no one agency knows about all the jobs.

Be responsive when the agency calls, and if you accept a temporary assignment, be sure to fulfill your obligation. Otherwise, you probably won't get another chance.

Dress for an interview when you visit the agency. You never know. You could be sent right over to a prospective employer.

AARP Works (AARP), 236
acceptance letters, 149–153
Advertising Age, 129
alumni associations, 132
American Almanac of Jobs and Salaries, The, 121
American Trade and Professional Associations Directory, The, 123–124,
    126
Amway, 77
Artistic interest categories (Strong Interest Inventory), 28–30, 44–45
Associated Press, 120
awards, including in résumés, 176

Baby Boomers, 120
Batchelder, David, 129
Ben and Jerry's Ice Cream, 77
Bill and Melinda Gates Foundation, 117
body language, 200
Bolles, Richard, 49, 131
Breen, Paul, 63–65
Briggs, Katherine, 89
Briggs-Myers, Isabel, 89
Business Week magazine, 129

California
    Economically Displaced Workers Assistance Act, 236
    Job Match, 236
Career Architect, 237
Career Builder (Web site), 116
career centers/career counselors, 27, 121, 242, 252
career change, 15–18
    assessing goals for, 250–252
    estimated time line for, 244–245
    goals for, 25–26
    personality style and, 89–90, 137
    work values and, 69
"career consumers," 116, 197
Career Development Team, 11
Career Journal (Web site), 116
career objectives, in résumés, 163, 165–170, 178
career research, 113–114, 116. *see also* Professional Self model
    decision making about, 134–135
    of employers, 128–131
    global trends and, 117–119

industry trends and, 121–125
informational interviews for, 131–134
national trends and, 119–121
of specific positions, 125–128
types of resources for, 115–117
chambers of commerce, 131
China, 117–118
civil engineering, 121
clarification letters, 149–151, 228–229
Codes of Ethics, 77
Collegiate Employment Research Institute, 47
communication skills, 63
cultural factors in interviews and, 198–202
personality style and, 85
Complete Job-Search Handbook, The (Figler), 67
Conventional interest categories (Strong Interest Inventory), 28–30, 45
corporate values, 76–78
correspondence, 141
acceptance/rejection/counteroffer letters, 152–156, 220–221
clarification letters, 149–152, 228–229
cover letters, 141–145
industry-specific materials and, 161–162
query letters, 156–158
questionnaires, 158–161
thank-you letters, 145–148
counteroffer letters, 152–156, 221
critical thinking skills, 64
cultural factors, in interviews, 198–202

Danna, Jo, 177
demographics, 120–121
design and planning skills, 64
Directory of Information Resources in the U.S., A., 127

Economically Displayed Workers Assistance Act, 236
economic trends, career research and, 117–119, 120
editing, of résumés, 179–181
Editor & Publisher, 129
education, including in résumés, 178–179
electronic résumés, 174, 175–176, 186–188
emotional values, 67
employer research, 128–131
employment agencies, 218, 253–255
Encyclopedia of Associations and Organizations, The, 126
Erdlen, Jack, 237

Erdlen Bograd Group, 237
executive search firms, 254
experience
    conveying in interviews, 194–195
    including in résumés, 169–174
    skills identification and, 56–58
    in volunteer activities, 58–59
Extroverts (Myers-Briggs personality type), 90–91, 92, 107

Feeling type (Myers-Briggs personality type), 90, 93–94, 108–100
Feingold, S. Norman, 123
"50–30–20 rule," of job proficiency, 197
Figler, Howard, 51, 67, 164
Frankel, Viktor E., 7–8
Fuchs, Richard, 170
functional-style résumés, 174, 175–176, 182–183

Gardner, Phillip, 3, 47
global economic/political trends, 117–119
goals
    for career, 11–14, 19–20, 250–252
    changing, 25–26
    for job search, 240–243

"headhunters," 254
High Tech Jobs for Non Tech Graduates, 127
Hispanic Business Magazine, 129
hobbies, including in résumés, 176
Holland, John
    Making Vocational Choice, 26
    occupational themes of, 43–45
    Self-Directed Search, 27
human relations and interpersonal skills, 64

Inc. magazine, 129
industry-specific materials, for job search, 161–162
industry trends, career research in, 121–125
informational interviews, 131–134, 158–161
information management skills, 63
interest inventory, 23–26
    occupational themes for, 43–45
    Personality/Interest Inventory, 37–41
    Strong Interest Inventory (SII) for, 26–30
    visualization of dream job and, 30–35

interviews, 189–195
    attributes sought by employers in, 213–214
    communicating strengths in, 198–202
    conducting research for, 195–198
    conveying self-confidence in, 202
    establishing experience/skills in, 194–195
    frequently asked questions in, 211–212
    preparing for, 202–207, 208–210
    references and, 207–208
Introverts (Myers-Briggs personality type), 90–91, 92, 107
Intuitive type (Myers-Briggs personality types), 90, 93, 108
Investigative interest categories (Strong Interest Inventory), 28–30, 43

job duties, logging, 56
Job Match (California), 236
job search, 18–19
    balancing other activities with, 243
    continuing employment during, 235–236
    establishing schedule for, 233–235
    networking and, 236–238
    setting goals for, 240–241
    time line for active job seekers, 246–248
    time line for career change, 244
    transitioning to new field and, 238–240
Job Service (Kansas), 232
job training, 3
Judging type (Myers-Briggs personality type), 90, 94, 109
Jung, C. G., 88–89

Kansas Job Service, 236
Karli & Associates, 170
Kennedy, Joyce Lain, 175
Kennedy, Marilyn Moats, 170
Knock 'em Dead: With Great Answers to Interview Questions (Yate), 196
Kravetz, Gary, 209, 254

Lafevre, John L., 199
Lauber, Daniel, 127
leadership, 57–58
Leer, Sam, 6
Lemke, Jim, 175
letters. see correspondence
libraries, for career research, 115–117, 122–123

lifestyle
    balancing job search with, 241–242
    work and, 14–15
livelihood, 5–6

magazines, for career research, 115–117, 129
Making Vocational Choice (Holland), 26, 43–45
management and administration skills, 64
Man's Search for Meaning (Frankel), 7–8
marketing, 19. *see also* Professional Self model
    correspondence, 141–162
    developing tools for, 138
    interviewing and, 189–214
    job search and, 18–19, 233–248
    résumés, 163–188
Mary Kay, 77
material values, 67
Megatrends (Naisbitt), 249
Michelozzi, Betty Neville, 27
Miller, Norma Reno, 123
mission statements, 77
Myers-Briggs Type Indicator (MBTI), 88–91. *see also* personality style
    personality types, 92–96, 107–109
    work dynamics and, 96–99

Naisbitt, John, 249
National Association of Colleges and Employers (NACE), 51–52, 213
National Career Choices, 209, 254
national economic/political trends, 119–121
natural disasters, impact on careers, 122
negotiating, 217–230
    common negotiable items, 230
    discussing requirements, 218–220
    evaluating counteroffer and, 223–224
    identifying decision makers and, 220–221
    identifying road blocks and, 225–228
    presenting plan and, 220–221
    written reply to offers and, 149–152, 220, 228–229
networking, 132, 236–238
New Emerging Careers: Today, Tomorrow and in the 20th Century (Feingold, Miller), 124
New Options Program, 194
newspapers, for career research, 115–117, 129
nongovernmental organizations (NGOs), 117
nonprofit organizations, 133

Occupational Outlook Handbook, 123
occupational themes, 43–45
Opportunities in ... (VGA book series), 125

Patagonia Industries, 77
Peek Inside the Recruiter's Briefcase, A (Lafevre), 199
Perceiving type (Myers-Briggs personality type), 90, 94–95, 109
personal and career development skills, 65
personal assessment
    determining work values for, 67–84
    establishing job search time line and, 233
    identifying skills for, 47–65, 194–195, 213–214
    importance of, 21
    interest inventory for, 23–45
personality style and, 85–109
Professional Self model for, 3–21, 53, 89–90, 118, 137, 234
Personality/Interest Inventory, 37–41
personality style, 85–88
    Myers-Briggs Type Indicator (MBTI) and, 88–96, 107–109
    Myers-Briggs Type Indicator (MBTI) and work dynamics, 96–99
Personal Style Inventory, 100–105
personal management skills, 51–52
Personal Style Inventory (exercise), 100–105
perspective
    on career, 9–10
    career research and, 118
Philanthropy Today, 129
political trends, career research and, 117–121
portfolio of work samples, 158–160
practice, for interviews, 204
preparation, for interviews, 202–207, 208–210. *see also* research and
    investigation skills
professional organizations
    for career research, 126
    including in résumés, 176
Professional Self model, 3–4, 118, 137
    attitude toward career and, 7–9
    career research and, 137
    changing career and, 15–18
    defined, 4–7
    goals for career, 11–14, 19–20
    job search and, 18–19
    lifestyle and work, 14–15
    marketing and, 19

personal assessment and, 21, 234
personality style and, 89–90
perspective on career, 9–10
    skills identification and, 53
Professionals' Job Finder (Lauber), 127
Psychological Assessment Resources, Inc., 27
Publishers Weekly, 129

"quarterlife crisis," 9, 17
query letters, 156–158
questionnaires, 158–161
questions, frequently asked in interviews, 211–212
Quinn, Jane Bryant, 237

Reader's Guide to Periodical Literature, 122
recession, impact on careers, 119–120
references, 148, 208
rejection letters, 152–156
research and investigation skills, 63
    for interviews, 195–198
    for salary negotiation, 218–220
résumés, 19, 163–167
    career objectives in, 167–169
    editing of, 179–181
    education included in, 178–179
    examples, 182–183, 184 185, 186–188
    experience history in, 176
    format for, 174–176
    nonessentials included in, 176–178
    skills/experience/accomplishments in, 169–174
retraining, work values and, 69–70

self-confidence, 201–202
Self-Directed Search (Holland), 27
self-esteem, 8
Sensing type (Myers-Briggs personality type), 90, 93, 107–108
September 11, 2001 (9/11) terrorist attacks, 120
Sims, Kathy, 9
skills, 47–50, 60–62
    attributes sought by employers, 213–214
    classification of, 63–65
    conveying in interviews, 194–195
    experience and, 56–59

Skills Vocabulary exercise for, 53–56
    types of, 50–52
social values, 67
spiritual values, 67
Standard and Poor's, 122
Standard Directory of Advertisers (Standard Rate and Data Service, Inc.), 126
Standard Rate and Data Service, Inc., 126
Strong Interest Inventory (SII), 26–30
Sturman, Gerald M., 11

technical/work knowledge skills, 51
temporary job assignments, 238, 253–255
terrorism, impact on careers, 120
thank-you letters, 145–148
Thinking types (Myers-Briggs personality type), 90, 93, 108
time line examples
    for active job seekers, 246–248
    for career change, 244–245
trade agreements, 117
traditional chronological-style résumés, 174–176, 184–185
transferable skills, 50–51
"two head test," interviews as, 192

Ugoline, Benita, 237
unifying principles, 68
U.S. Bureau of Labor Statistics, 124
U.S. Census Bureau, 121
U.S. Industrial Outlook (U.S. Department of Labor), 123

Values Prioritization exercise, 79–83
valuing skills, 63
visualization, of dream job, 30–35
vocabulary
    Skills Vocabulary exercise, 53–56
    used for résumés, 173
volunteer experience, skills identification and, 58–59

wardrobe, 208–209
Web sites, for career research, 115–117
Western Staff Services, 255
What Color Is Your Parachute (Bolles), 49, 131
Whitaker, Urban, 63–65
Wineapple, Maxine, 194

Winning the Job Interview Game: Tips for the High Tech Era (Danna), 177
Wood, Cris, 255
work experience. *see* experience
Working Woman (magazine), 124
work values, 67–71, 84
    choices in, 71–74
    clarifying, 71
    corporate values and, 76–78
    plan of action for, 74–76
    Values Prioritization exercise, 79–83
writing samples, 159–160

Yate, Martin, 196

Zwicke, Onolee, 199